A Free Man of Color

Plays by John Guare

Bosoms and Neglect

Chaucer in Rome

Cop-Out

A Few Stout Individuals

Four Baboons Adoring the Sun

A Free Man of Color

General of Hot Desire

His Girl Friday (adaptation)

Home Fires

House of Blue Leaves

Lake Hollywood

Landscape of the Body

Lydie Breeze:
Part One: Women and Water
Part Two: Bulfinch's Mythology
Part Three: The Sacredness of the Next Task

Marco Polo Sings a Solo

Moon Under Miami

Muzeeka

Rich and Famous

Six Degrees of Separation

JOHN GUARE

A Free Man of Color

Grove Press
New York

For
George C. Wolfe who put it into motion,
André Bishop and Bernard Gersten who made it happen,
and Adele C-T who gave it the spirit

A Free Man of Color was commissioned and produced by the Lincoln Center Theater at the Vivian Beaumont, New York, New York, under the direction of André Bishop and Bernard Gersten. It opened in December 2010 with the following cast:

JACQUES CORNET   Jeffrey Wright

CUPIDON MURMUR AND TOUSSAINT LOUVERTURE   Mos

ZEUS-MARIE PINCEPOUSSE AND TALLYRAND   Reg Rogers

MARGERY JOLICOEUR   Nicole Beharie

DR. TOUBIB   Joseph Marcell

JUAN VENTURA MORALES AND NAPOLEON BONAPARTE   Triney Sandoval

DOÑA SMERALDA AND JOSEPHINE   Justina Machado

ORPHEE   Esau Pritchett

LEDA, MME. DORILANTE, AND MELPOMENE   Teyonah Parris

DOÑA ATHENE AND CALLIOPE   Sara Gettelfinger

REMY DORILANTE AND JAMES MONROE   Arnie Burton

JONATHAN SPARKS AND MAJOR WALTER REED   Brian Reddy

MRS. SPARKS, TERPSICHORE, AND THE INFANTA   Rosal Colón

LORD HARCOURT, LE CLERC'S CAPTAIN, AND GEORGES FEYDEAU   Robert Stanton

LADY HARCOURT AND EUTERPE   Wendy Rich Stetson

ALCIBIADE   David Emerson Toney

PYTHAGORE, GENERAL LE CLERC AND KING CARLOS CUARTO   Nick Mennell

MERCURE AND COUNT ACHILLE CREUX   Peter Bartlett

MME. MANDRAGOLA, DOÑA POLISSENA, AND ROBERT
LIVINGSTON   Veanne Cox

THOMAS JEFFERSON   John McMartin

MERIWETHER LEWIS   Paul Dano

Director   George C. Wolfe
Sets   David Rockwell
Costumes   Ann Hould-Ward
Lighting   Jules Fisher and Peggy Eisenhauer
Sound   Scott Stauffer
Original Music   Jeanine Tesori
Choreography   Hope Clarke

The play is set in New Orleans, 1801–1806, and other locations
in Europe and America.

In the New World at this time, there was a vocabulary of more
than a hundred terms for people of mixed race, extending back
seven generations in an individual's heritage. For example: "pure"
white and "pure" black = mulatto; mulatto and black = sambo;
mulatto and white = quadroon; a mamelouc was "113 of 120
parts white," etc.

ACT ONE

JACQUES CORNET *appears, a dazzling piece of work. His coat is made of purple satin and embroidered and laced with gold. His shoes have diamond buckles. His bewigged hair, powdered. His magnificence is overwhelming.* MURMUR *accompanies him.*

JACQUES   The year is 1801. Alas. This is the last time men will
dress like this.
   All men equal? Clothes tell the ranks.
   I have taste. For that I give my daily thanks.
   If a book can't be told by its cover, what good's the book?
   The world would be better if it followed my lead.
   If I'm a book, I'm a damned good read.
   Murmur, introduce me—

MURMUR   His name used to be—

JACQUES CORNET *(cutting him off)*   My name is Jacques
Cornet. New Orleans is my home.

MURMUR   I'm Cupidon Murmur, his administrative assistant.

JACQUES CORNET   Last time I looked, you were my slave.

MURMUR   Which is why I stopped looking. Didn't you used to
be a slave?

JACQUES CORNET   Don't be fresh, Murmur. Even though born
of a slave, I purchased my freedom and became my father's
heir.

MURMUR   'My father's heir.' A very rich, very white father, left
my boss everything. Including me. I do all the work. He does
nothing.

JACQUES CORNET   I beg your pardon. Each morning I can be
found in my atelier, writing my play.

MURMUR   Where'd you get the nerve to write a play?

JACQUES CORNET Brocade gave me confidence.

MURMUR Does your masterpiece have a title?

JACQUES CORNET *A Free Man of Color.*

MURMUR What would it be about?

JACQUES CORNET The sanctity of surfaces. The value of
veneer.
Lift the curtain. We begin.
Lift the curtain. Is being deaf your latest claim?

MURMUR I thought you'd like to know some crates just came.

JACQUES CORNET Crates? Get them! You slow beast!
Freedom's not for you.

MURMUR What happened to the show must go on?

Murmur rolls in wooden crates.

JACQUES CORNET A shipment has arrived! Persia! Asia Minor!
My only prayer some evil moth
hasn't gnawed his way through sacred cloth.
Open, Murmur!

MURMUR *(opening crates)* I'm hurrying! I'm hurrying!

JACQUES CORNET Look—grosgrain for trimming!
Bolts of cloth never come with regret.
Ahh! To be tickled by the feather of an egret.
What genius hands in Samarkand wove this silk,
encasing my legs like a glove in milk.
The legs are so important. Revere their line,
especially with a golden calf as shapely as mine.
Poor innocent silks—suppose you were lost!
How many years did your treacherous voyage cost?

MURMUR Here's a date! They left Shanghai in 1798!

JACQUES CORNET   Three years for silk to travel? I could have frozen to death. Bring out my maps! Unveil my maps!

Which Murmur does. The maps glow.

MURMUR   He collects these maps—

JACQUES CORNET   Murmur, know your place. I collect these maps. One of them must reveal the magic route to deliver me the treasures that I need like bread and water. The future is always about speed. That's the true subject of my play. An inland river must cross this vast unknown land. A river from the isle of California that somehow meets the Mississippi— but where? It has to be there. The stakes are too high. (*Jacques starts to undress.*)
   The iridescence of this pink moiré
   will dazzle the fools who flock to my soirée.
   Murmur, undo this cuff. Murmur, remove this shoe.
   Take these crates to my chamber. Faster! Faster!

MURMUR   Yes, master master.
(*to us*)
   I'm taking up a collection to buy my freedom. Spare change?

JACQUES CORNET   Murmur! Open the curtain or I'll damn you to perdition.

MURMUR   Don't the dumbest plays need exposition?

JACQUES CORNET   My play speaks for itself.

MURMUR   I'll tell them what they need to know.

JACQUES CORNET   I wouldn't trust you as far as a rat might speed.
   Dr. Toubib? Tell them what truths they need.

Jacques Cornet goes, trailing clothes, which Murmur picks up.
DR. TOUBIB *enters, of African descent, a man of reason.*

3

MURMUR This is Dr. Toubib. He ministers to the health of the town. One day I'll write a play. Act One, Scene One.

Murmur lifts the curtain and wheels off the crates.

Music plays: Haydn trio in G major 3rd movement.
REMY DORILANTE, JONATHAN SPARKS, LORD SIDNEY HARCOURT, and ACHILLE ALCIBIADE, *and* MME. MANDRAGOLA *play Faro, a card game.*

DR. T The home of Jacques Cornet on the Rue de la Levée in New Orleans. Every Tuesday, he opens his home to men who come selling maps that might unmask the unmapped continent and get his clothes here quicker.

Murmur deals cards at the faro table.

DORILANTE I mase double.

MME MANDRAGOLA I set that.

SPARKS Mase double again!

MME MANDRAGOLA I set that and I win.

DR. T No one comes to the new world because they want to. This one's been deported, this one disinherited, this one escaped the police. They spy, steal, smuggle, sometimes even work honestly, until the day their fortune will surely appear. They come to the house of Jacques Cornet to gamble what little they have. Double it. Triple it.

MURMUR Or lose it to Jacques Cornet. The cards are fixed. My boss leaves nothing to chance.

DR. T Today is Tuesday, February 24th—the feast of Mardi Gras. The few social barriers that exist in New Orleans are down tonight—white—black—everything in between—

MURMUR —and there's a lot of in between.

4

DR. T Take off your twenty-first century glasses. See New Orleans as we who live here see it in 1801. The free-est city in the world. Imagine the unimaginable. Race is a celebration! See the lush palette of skin tones in New Orleans.

DORILANTE Remy Dorilante. I am a shade called *Meamelouc* —white and *metif.*

SPARKS Jonathan Sparks! I'm *Quarteron*—white and *meamelouc.*

HARCOURT Lord Sidney Harcourt. I send furs from Quebec down the Mississippi to New Orleans and out to the world. I'm truly white, which gives me no privilege. Here it's just another color.

ALCIBIADE (*heavy Norwegian accent*) Achille Alcibiade from Norway. I have come to New Orleans to start a new life as a dealer in furniture. I am white.

MURMUR How come you look like a mahogany table?

ALCIBIADE All right—not Norway. Barbados. (*back to the accent*) But in New Orleans you can be whatever you declare yourself to be.

JUAN VENTURA MORALES *bangs on the bedroom door. He's quite chubby, dressed in some sort of gold armor.*

MORALES I command you to open this door for Juan Ventura Morales, appointed by His Royal Majesty Carlos Cuarto, King of Spain, as the Supreme Intendante of New Orleans.

MURMUR Tax collector.

MORALES I am Castilian! Pure blood!

MURMUR His maternal grandmother had a touch of the brush.

MORALES Among other divinely ordained powers by the kingdom of Spain, I control travel on the Mississippi.

DR. T The Mississippi being North America's link to the world.

MME. MANDRAGOLA (*to us*)   I am Mme Mandragola. From Buenos Aires. Like Joseph in the Bible, I am a coat of many colors. I supply New Orleans with the comfort of the most luscious kaleidoscope of flesh.

From behind the bedroom door we hear:

GIRLS (*off*)   Ohh! Ohhhhh! Ohhhhhhh! Jacques, Jacques, Jacques!

MORALES   Why do you let Jacques Cornet hoard your girls?

MME. MANDRAGOLA   He has more money than any of you. Are you going to the Mardi Gras ball tonight?

MORALES   I already have on my costume.

MME. MANDRAGOLA   Are you Sancho Panza?

MORALES   I am *El Cid*! The greatest hero Spain has ever known! And I am a direct descendant! (*knocking on Jacques's door*)   Have some consideration. I can't keep my wife waiting.

The door to the bedroom opens. Mme. Mandragolas girls appear, en dishabille. TERPSICHORE (Terp-sikor), CALLIOPE (Kal-ee-Ope) EUTERPE (You terp) MELPOMENE (mel-pom-eeen). They run to the table and eat hungrily.

MORALES   Finally! Murmur, find me a *chambre d'amour*. Presto!

EUTERPE   No! This is just a break to catch my breath. I am Euterpe—

CALLIOPE   Calliope—

TERPSICHORE   Terpsichore—

MELPOMENE   Melpomene—

6

MME. MANDRAGOLA (*to us*)   We locals name ourselves after Greek gods and demi-gods and muses but give it a French twist.

MORALES (*to Terpsichore*)   I have decided to honor you with my body.

TERPSICHORE   Sorry! I've just experienced the greatest happiness of my life and don't want to ruin it.

MORALES   Common whores refuse the Supreme Intendante of New Orleans?

TERPSICHORE   Put me in jail. Jacques Cornet has a key that unlocks the world. Dr. T, what's the Latin word for key?

DR. T   *Clavis!*

TERPSICHORE   I am the portal. Jacques Cornet is the *clavis*.

CALLIOPE   Imagine the arm of a needy five year old reaching out to you, holding a bright red juicy apple—

MELPOMENE   —the neck of a flamingo flying home—and you're the *nest*.

EUTERPE   —the trunk of a mandingo tree that goes up, up, up and at the top, there's a gorgeous red blossom flowering.

They sigh.

MORALES   I could show you a thing or two.

THE WHORES   You have!

MORALES   Like the present size of the United States, I'm perfectly happy with what I've got. (*beats on Jacques' door*) Cornet, you will pay for your disrespect!

ZEUS-MARIE PINCEPOUSSE *appears, ignored by all.*

PINCEPOUSSE (*to us*)   I am Zeus-Marie Pincepousse.

MURMUR   Who the hell invited you?

PINCEPOUSSE (*pushing Murmur aside*)   I am extremely white and my blood extremely blue. I hate being in this house, which is rightfully mine.

MURMUR   He is half-brother to Jacques Cornet. They share the same white father.

PINCEPOUSSE   But my mother was a *Duchesse*. His mother a mere possession. I am also the plot. I'll be back.

Pincepousse goes. Murmur fills everyone's wine glass.

HARCOURT   Murmur, I heard news of a rebellion upriver on your master's sugar farm.

MURMUR   Yes, we caught wind of that rumor. Peace was restored.

SPARKS   How did you deal with it?

MURMUR   I shot the instigator.

DORILANTE   You shot a slave?

MURMUR   Not my first.

HARCOURT   But you're a slave.

MURMUR   What does that have to do with it?

DORILANTE   Suppose you ran away?

MURMUR   But I wouldn't.

HARCOURT   Do you want to be free?

MURMUR   You bet.

SPARKS   And what would you do if you could be free?

MURMUR   Work for Jacques Cornet.

Jacques appears in the doorway of his bedroom in a silken robe. He tosses gold to Mme. Mandragola.

JACQUES CORNET   Ladies! Round Two!

SPARKS   Jacques, see the treasures I've brought!

DORILANTE   I've painted your portrait! Jacques!

HARCOURT   Jacques! See my map!

Jacques shuts the door. PYTHAGORE, *wearing a black mask, a bone in his nose, leaps at Morales.*

PYTHAGORE   I am Toussaint Louverture and I want freedom!

MORALES (*screams*)   Take everything I have! Don't hurt me!

PYTHAGORE (*unmasking himself*)   It's Pythagore. I thought my Mardi Gras costume amusing.

SPARKS   You wouldn't joke if you'd just returned from (*whispers*)   Santo Domingo.

MORALES   Not so loud—The very mention of that bloody island will cause chaos here in New Orleans. We must keep the news from the slaves. I'd suggest you find a less provocative costume for tonight.

DR. T   *Sante Domingue.* The richest island in the Caribbean and soon to be named Haiti. Toussaint Louverture, after a long bloody battle, has finally taken control of the island from the French planters and is declared governor-general for life of this new sovereign nation.

TOUSSAINT LOUVERTURE *appears.*

TOUSSAINT   Behold this land, which we have watered with our blood. We, humble victims, were ready for anything, not wishing at first to abandon our master who gave us freedom. We were mistaken; those who, next to God, should have proved our fathers, had become tyrants, monsters, unworthy of the fruits of our labors. God, who fights for the innocent,

9

is our guide; he will never abandon us. Accordingly this is our motto—victory or death for freedom!

DR. T   But the French planters have not given up. Toussaint may be the Bonaparte of *Sante Domingo* but he still needs outside support to maintain control.

TOUSSAINT   Hear me, glorious first consul Bonaparte, from the first of the blacks to the first of the whites, I know you will give our new government the supplies we urgently need!

DR. T   Napoleon's not emperor yet. He's still first consul, pulling France together after her revolution. Let me take you to the heart of it—Paris—to the Tuilleries, a malodorous palace along side the Louvre. The same question Jacques Cornet asks of how to get to the Orient torments Napoleon.

Enter NAPOLEON in a bathtub, studying a terry cloth map of the world.

NAPOLEON   The route to India through Egypt should be mine. But the British stopped me. I will retaliate. But how!

DR. T   Josephine, his wife, not yet Empress, enters.

JOSEPHINE *enters, with tarot cards.*

JOSEPHINE *(distraught)*   Look at my clothes—I am laughed at—spots on my muslin.

NAPOLEON   Then wash them and leave me alone. How? How?

JOSEPHINE   Wash them in Paris? Only the water of the West Indies possesses magic bubbles to make my muslin gleam like teeth!

NAPOLEON   We have no money to go to the West Indies for your laundry or your teeth.

JOSEPHINE   Oh, but if England's involved, you spend any amount to defeat them, but little Josephine wants one little spot taken out of her muslin and Citizen Big Shot First Consul cries poverty. (*dealing tarot cards*)   Money, money. That's a laugh.

Toussaint enters, writing a letter.

TOUSSAINT   Come to the West Indies and enforce the ideals of the Revolution!

TALLEYRAND *enters, bearing the letter.*

DR. T   Toussaint's letter arrives months later into the hands of Talleyrand, Napoleon's foreign minister. Talleyrand is known fondly in diplomatic circles as 'a silk stocking crammed with shit'.

TALLYRAND   Destiny smiles yet again on Talleyrand. I can parlay this to my advantage—(*Tallyrand hands the letter to Napolean*)   Magnificent Beacon of Destiny, our future has arrived.

NAPOLEON (*scanning the letter, discarding the letter*)   Aside from putting sugar in my morning coffee, the West Indies hold no interest for me—

TALLYRAND   Savior of France, don't you see what this could be? An entry into America!

JOSEPHINE (*reading the letter*)   These savages wash their clothes in West Indies water, but me—covered with spots like a Dalmatian dog—

NAPOLEON   GO!

TALLYRAND   Feel the future pulsate.

NAPOLEON   The Nile.

TALLYRAND   The Mississippi. The river to the Orient surely lies here within America. This vast unknown covers volcanoes spewing gold.

JOSEPHINE (*dealing her cards*)   Yet again 'money'. Can tarot lie?

NAPOLEON   How to crush Great Britain?

TALLYRAND   Say it, oh Jewel of the Future: England has defeated me.

NAPOLEON   No! If the Gargantua of England cannot defeat the mouse of their colonies, how can England defeat the splendor of me?

TALLYRAND   And yet they have! Sail to America.

NAPOLEON   The British would attack me at sea. I hate the British. I hate Shakespeare. I hate Chaucer. I hate Richard the Lion Hearted. I hate Henry V. When the future comes, I will hate Big Ben. Queen Victoria. James Bond. Charles Dickens. Florence Nightingale. British Air. Julie Andrews. Mick Jagger. No. I will like him. Wait! I see how to crush Great Britain! (*Napoleon stands up in the tub. Instead of a penis, he sports a giant cannon*)   I'll conquer Europe. I'll humiliate the British as they have humiliated me. Never mention America again.

Napoleon goes.

Music: the Arcangelo Corelli Concerto Grosso # 2 in F major. THOMAS JEFFERSON *wearing a bathrobe and slippers appears, playing his Cremona violin. He surveys the unopened crates.*

DR. T   Presenting Thomas Jefferson, the third president of the small, perfectly sized, sixteen United States.

JEFFERSON   Where is the *Medoc?* (*calls*)   Meriwether? Meriwether! Where is the *Medoc?*

DR. T   Mr. Jefferson's first full day on the job after a very contentious election. Enter Meriwether Lewis, personal secretary to Mr. Jefferson.

MERIWETHER LEWIS, *twenty-something, enters, harried, carrying lots of mail.*

MERIWETHER   Sir! We just got word. New Hampshire is building a fort on land Canada claims is Canadian. What are the borders?

JEFFERSON   A state's business is none of a government's business. Send them a letter reminding them—

MERIWETHER   I don't have time to write letters—

JEFFERSON   And make twelve copies of it—

MERIWETHER   Sir! So many men would do this job better than I.

JEFFERSON   Any other news?

Toussaint appears.

TOUSSAINT   My country needs your assistance.

MERIWETHER   Yes! Yes! The Indies. Toussaint Louverture requesting materiel—

TOUSSAINT   Food, ammunition—

MERIWETHER   —to fight the French planters—

TOUSSAINT   Give us what you would give a young democracy struggling for the same freedom—

TOUSSAINT & MERIWETHER   as you once did.

MERIWETHER   Sir, I must return to my life outdoors.

JEFFERSON *(impatient)*   American news?

MERIWETHER   James Callender writes unless you appoint him postmaster of Richmond, Virginia, he'll publish trouble in his newspaper about Sally Hemmings.

JEFFERSON   I dare him! Open that crate.

MERIWETHER (*opening the crate*) The two of us alone in this big, empty, unfinished house. Why do you even want me for this job? Sir, I need to be out in the white spaces! If I went to St. Louis and set out on the Missouri River—

JEFFERSON I'm not spending money on land that belongs to another country.

MERIWETHER Spain won't know I'm there.

JEFFERSON I'll know you're there.

MERIWETHER One canoe! That's all I need!

JEFFERSON The government does not have the money to send you out into this alien whiteness in even one canoe.

MERIWETHER You could charge it the way you do your wine.

JEFFERSON Run a country the way I conduct my personal life? Never.

MERIWETHER It makes me weep to think I'm to sit here cataloging the temperature of each day and taking notes on the workings of this government when there's this unknown alabaster out there! Did God create a continent and then cover its majority with a bafflement of snow? Does a mammoth beast, cruel as the Angel of Night, lurk out there, guarding the secret of the western route, devouring all explorers who are foolhardy enough to challenge him?

JEFFERSON You're talking yourself into a frenzy.

MERIWETHER To find the hidden river, connecting the Atlantic and the Pacific, the East to the West. The Indies! Christopher Columbus, Captain Cook, Magellan can finally sleep rested. Their task accomplished.

JEFFERSON By you.

MERIWETHER   Why not? To be out there in the limitless unknown looking for the future. I want to decipher what is unknown.

JEFFERSON (*stops playing*)   If you want the unknowable, get a wife.

MERIWETHER (*drinks*)   I'd rather climb in bed with my maps.

JEFFERSON (*handing Meriwether a list*)   Before you retire, make place cards, I'm having a dinner party tonight. Seat me next to Aaron Burr.

MERIWETHER   Your vice president hates you!

JEFFERSON   Opposite me, place Alexander Hamilton!

MERIWETHER   He wants to overthrow you.

JEFFERSON   They won't assassinate me my first night in my new home. That's not good manners. Drink up, my boy. To democracy!

MERIWETHER   Is the definition of democracy dining with your enemies?

JEFFERSON   That's the definition of life. As for Toussaint—

MERIWETHER   Sir, fair is fair. Their government's legal.

JEFFERSON   Yes, but I've heard the fears in Virginia. Those negroes of Toussaint will conduct predatory raids on our coasts and cause unrest. However—God knows my morning Santo Dominguin coffee needs two teaspoons of Santo Dominguin sugar. Democracy and America's sweet teeth cry out: Yes! Send Toussaint what he needs. Let's get back to my dinner party.

MERIWETHER   What about my request?

JEFFERSON   Tell the chef I want a light repast of turkey, chicken fricassee, mutton chops, ham, oysters, that pie called Macaroni!

MERIWETHER How will you pay for it?

JEFFERSON Charge it!

MERIWETHER Sir, I quit!

Jefferson goes, playing his violin. Meriwether follows.

Dr. T appears.

DR. T Back in New Orleans, Jacques is about to die a little death.

Morales has his ear to Jacques' bedroom door.

WHORES (*off*) AHHHHH
AHHHHH

MORALES I hear him—he's finishing!

A cannon goes off. The men snap into action.

MORALES He's finished!

MURMUR Get in line!

DORILANTE I was here first.

HARCOURT Liar! I was here first.

DORILANTE Your insult forces me to say 'Name your weapon'!

HARCOURT Your insult forces me to pick up my pistol and—

Jacques Cornet appears, dressed in full Sun King dazzle. The Girls follow.

JACQUES CORNET Please! Any duels shall take place in Lake Pontchartrain in six feet of water, sledge hammers to be used as weapons.

Everyone laughs merrily.

DORILANTE/SPARKS/HARCOURT/ALCIBIADE/PYTHAGORE See my map! Mine! Mine! Mine!

JACQUES CORNET I have that map—and that—

DORILANTE (*holding out a map*) Wonderful Jacques, no one has seen this map proving the Mississippi bends west—

JACQUES CORNET West? Don't make sport of gravity. Next.

ALCIBIADE Oh most delightful host, an Indian on his deathbed gave this to me.

PYTHAGORE As a dying Indian gave me *this* map with *his* last breath.

JACQUES CORNET Every map attached to a dead Indian? There can't be an Indian left alive. Murmur, buy them.

Harcourt shoves his map in front of Jacques Cornet.

HARCOURT My greatest friend, look!

JACQUES CORNET But this map was stolen from me!

HARCOURT Murmur!

MURMUR I never saw this map!

JACQUES CORNET Is this how you buy your freedom? Good! I take what I pay Harcourt for this map and add it to the sum you need to purchase your freedom. You keep stealing. I keep adding. I could never let you go. No map today, Sparks?

SPARKS Good Sire, I've lost every peso, every *real* at the gaming table. I have no way to explain this to my wife—

JACQUES CORNET Murmur? Pay good Sparks some of his losses. A real or two.

MURMUR His losses are none of your business.

JACQUES CORNET The difference between being a sport and a miser is the matter of only a few hundred pesos a year. I don't want his wife going hungry. She makes such a tasty meal.

SPARKS Some day I'll repay you.

Sparks kisses Jacques Cornet's hand.

JACQUES CORNET I look forward to the day.—Murmur, wash the hand.

MURMUR (*wiping Jacques Cornet's hand*) My master treats men like carnival dogs who roll over and fetch.

MERCURE, *a grizzled trapper, appears.*

JACQUES CORNET I've not seen you before.

MERCURE (*brandishing his map*) I have a map. I've been down here in the secret connector between the Atlantic and Pacific that runs underground! I entered through a cave in the Illinois territory—see—and sailed in dark caves—see—for many days until I spilled out into the Pacific's nacreous foam.

JACQUES CORNET Your breath.—This underground map is at least original. Pay him, Murmur.

Murmur does so. Mercure grovels with gratitude.

DR. T Why do you buy these maps?

JACQUES CORNET Like Pascal's wager regarding the existence of God, one of these maps just might be true.

MORALES (*trying to get Jacques Cornet's attention*) Most Exquisite Avatar of Beneficence, I compel you to command Señora Mandragola to allow me purchase the services of whichever of her girls I choose or I shall exile them to (*whispers*) Santo Domingo!

The Girls react in horror. NO!!!!

MME. MANDRAGOLA (*to Morales*) Which of my jewels do you want?

MORALES Melpomene.

MELPOMENE   NOOOOOO! M. Cornet! Save me! Don't you hear me? Sire, I implore you!

Melpomene inadvertently spills wine on Jacques Cornet's sleeve.

JACQUES CORNET   Horrors! A drop of wine! Destroy this jacket! Cruel silken death! Murmur, dress me once more—

Jacques Cornet and Murmur leave. Morales picks up Melpomene to go into the other room as—

DR. T   At this moment out in the harbor, a packet boat from Havana slithers into New Orleans. It bears a message from a spy in the court of the King of Spain, addressed to the *Supreme Intendante* Morales. It is marked TOP SECRET. And change, the ultimate unchartered territory, casts its latest devil-may-care map over everyone's head.

Pincepousse enters, agitated, out of breath, carrying an Imperial document.

PINCEPOUSSE (*gasping*)   Morales! There you are! A messenger came seeking you. I took the message. It's from Madrid. We never get mail.

MORALES   Pincepousse! I have a prior appointment. *Paciencia.*

Morales exits with Melpomene.

PINCEPOUSSE (*to us*)   The King of Spain probably wants Margery!

DR. T   Who is Margery?

PINCEPOUSSE   No one! (*to us*)   Margery Jolicoeur. My true love. The King of Spain has received word of my recent *plaçage* and wants her for his own. No! Margery is mine! 'She walks in beauty like the night'.

DR. T (*to us*) *Plaçage* is a local law allowing white men to enter into an official arrangement with a woman of color—it protects her—it protects him.

MURMUR Think of marriage without any of the downside.

Jacques enters in yet another dazzling outfit.

JACQUES CORNET My brother! You've been out of town.

PINCEPOUSSE My dear *half*-brother—Gad, I hate him so much I have forgot what I was going to say. All this should be mine!

JACQUES CORNET Is that a letter for me?

PINCEPOUSSE Not everything's for you. I'm waiting for Morales.

JACQUES CORNET The letter upsets you.

PINCEPOUSSE Nothing could be further from the truth. I revel in the serenity of my mother being a *Duchesse*.

Enter MARGERY JOLICOEUR, *dressed in country clothes and wearing a tignon, a scarf wrapped high on her head, decorated with jewels and flowers.*

MARGERY How long I got to wait in that drafty carriage?

PINCEPOUSSE (*a rage*) Wait in the carriage! Let no man see you.

JACQUES CORNET Is that a wife?

PINCEPOUSSE Yes. No! Not a wife!

MARGERY What beautiful dishes! What a beautiful house! (*she sees Jacques*) Oh. What a beautiful man.

JACQUES CORNET (*to Margery*) They told me you were beautiful. They didn't tell me you were this beautiful—

PINCEPOUSSE Wait in the carriage!

Pincepousse drags Margery out.

DORILANTE Pincepousse has already lost his wife.

HARCOURT I wouldn't let my wife near Jacques.

SPARKS Luckily, my wife has never seen Jacques.

MURMUR (*holding up a key ring heavy with keys, to us*) See these keys? My boss knows his way into these men's bedrooms.

Pincepousse returns, attempting nonchalance.

JACQUES CORNET Why, you old whore master, have you married? Murmur, bring the champagne!

PINCEPOUSSE I deny it! (*banging on the chamber door*) Morales!!!! —The young woman is—she is—not a woman. It was merely a young man in costume for the ball tonight.

JACQUES CORNET A boy in a dress? You are getting interesting in your old age. He was exceedingly pretty. Bring him in.

PINCEPOUSSE You shall not debauch her—him.

JACQUES CORNET You insist he's male? Have you foresworn the fairer sex?

PINCEPOUSSE I do have a mistress.

JACQUES CORNET And the young man? A *ménage a trois?*

PINCEPOUSSE No *ménage.* Only her—brother!

JACQUES CORNET Does your mistress know her brother is being seen around town in her clothes?

PINCEPOUSSE I don't know the fashion of the young.

JACQUES CORNET Let me make you a wedding gift.

PINCEPOUSSE I shall happily accept a wedding gift—such as this house, which is rightfully mine!

JACQUES CORNET   *After* I meet her. Bring her here.

PINCEPOUSSE   She's too awkward and ill-favored to bring to town. (*aside*)   He wants everything that is mine!

Morales opens the chamber door—a matador after a kill.

MORALES   Olè!

Melpomene follows, limping.

MELPOMENE   He kept his armor on.

PINCEPOUSSE (*pulls Morales aside*)   Look at this letter!

MORALES (*opens it; shock!*)   It's a cryptogram!

PINCEPOUSSE   A cryptogram?

MORALES   I remember some of the cipher. Plxtr is "Spain". Here is another—Voomf is "Napoleon".

JACQUES CORNET   Spain? Napoleon?

MORALES   Am I being dismissed? Oh, dear Lord—no—

PINCEPOUSSE   Where did you put the Imperial cipher breaker?

MORALES   At home in my safe.

PINCEPOUSSE (*whispers*)   Could the cryptogram be orders to restore *le Code Noir*? I'd like that.

JACQUES CORNET   What is he saying?

MORALES   Restore *le Code Noir*?

JACQUES CORNET   *Le Code Noir?* What about *le Code Noir?*

DR. T (*to us*)   George Feydeau, the great French playwright, was asked how to write a play.

GEORGES FEYDEAU *appears.*

FEYDEAU   There is only one rule of playwriting. Character A says "My life is perfect as long as Character B does not show up." Knock knock. Enter Character B.

Georges Feydeau goes.

JACQUES CORNET   My life is perfect.

Murmur enters, carrying a door. He is dressed in black and holds a skull.

MURMUR   Knock knock.

JACQUES CORNET   Who's there?

MURMUR/DEATH   *Le Code Noir!*

Jacques Cornet, terrified, slams the door shut. Murmur goes.

DR. T *(to us)*   He'll tell you what *le Code Noir* is later in a very grand speech.

MORALES   Jacques, *muchos gracias* for your hospitality.— Pincepousse, to my house. Let no one suspect we have received a cryptogram.

PINCEPOUSSE   Find the code breaker!

Margery enters.

MARGERY   I want to see New Orleans. I want to eat food. I want to see that man.

PINCEPOUSSE   The carriage! Go!

Pincepousse drags Margery off. Morales follows.

JACQUES CORNET   A restoration of *le Code Noir?* Spain lets us live in the mathematics of a loose equation. But add Napoleon to the algebra? The name of my play is very clear: *A Free Man of Color* or *The Happy Life of a Man in Power.*

What's in that letter? Murmur, bring me the key to the garden of Senor Morales. Hurry! Hurry!

MURMUR (*taking out the key ring*)   I'm hurrying.

Jacques Cornet goes onto the street. A masked woman appears.
(DOÑA ATHENE) *Jacques Cornet turns to her.*

JACQUES CORNET   They told me you were beautiful. They didn't tell me you—

DOÑA ATHENE (*pulls off mask*)   It is your *wife*! Doña Athene! Why have you scorned me!

JACQUES CORNET   Murmur!

MURMUR   I'm staying out of this one.

DOÑA ATHENE   I thought I would dwell in Paradise when you begged to marry me to celebrate your newly purchased freedom. I relented happily to the wonder of your words. You promised me Israel in your arms. You parted the Red Sea when you loved me. Now you deny me your ardor. Why would Moses turn his back on his chosen people? A Gethsemane of madness crushes in on me. Your phantom words divorce me from all sense. How can you speak, yet be devoid of consequence?

Jacques Cornet runs off.

DOÑA ATHENE   What did I do to make him turn away?

MURMUR   Take it as a compliment, Madam. He found such comfort in your arms that he seeks you everywhere.

DOÑA ATHENE   "The Increase of appetite had grown by what it feeds on." Is that my crime? My love made him discover love?

MURMUR   There you go.

Doña Athene goes. Jacques Cornet reappears.

JACQUES CORNET   Murmur, one of your few duties is to block Doña Athene.

MURMUR   She *is* your wife.

JACQUES CORNET   A moment's spur. I didn't buy myself out of one slavery to move into another. What's in that letter?

Murmur plays the seductive rhythm of el son *on a gourd.*

MURMUR   The drawing room of Supreme Intendante Juan Ventura Morales.

DOÑA SMERALDA, *the wife of Morales, sits with* ACHILLE CREUX *and his wife,* DONA POLISSENA, *who carries a microscope. A bedroom is visible.*
Morales and Pincepousse enter and proceed to take the drawing room apart.

MORALES   The safe! It's here—in this safe—

DOÑA SMERALDA   Darlingest treasure trove! We have company!

MORALES   Have you seen the Imperial decoder—parchment— sealed with red wax—in a black leather tube?

DOÑA SMERALDA   Darlingest jewel in my jewel box, your cousin has arrived from Santo Domingo!

CREUX   Juan Ventura!

MORALES (*turns, sees*)   Achille!

They embrace.

CREUX   Toussaint Louverture and his black beasts left *Sante Domingue* a desert. We once sweetened the world. Now my fertile island is a burned-out crater on a distant moon.

DOÑA POLISSENA   We made our way through the flames of our plantation to *Port Ste. Dauphine*, found a ship about to sail for New Orleans. Two weeks later, *voila!*

PINCEPOUSSE We all have our problems. Could it be in the stables?

They exit.

DOÑA SMERALDA Our joy to offer safety. Let our slaves fetch your things.

CREUX Things?! We who had jewels and pianofortes and portraits of ancestors such as Charlemagne, Caligula, and Pontius Pilate, sailed out of Sante Domingue carrying only identity papers.

DOÑA POLISSENA I, taking only my microscope.

DOÑA SMERALDA Microscope?

CREUX My wife charmingly describes herself as a scientist.

DOÑA POLISSENA I *am* a scientist! My dream is to find the cause of yellow fever. Could it be that grape?

CREUX We all know yellow fever is caused by Negroes who touch us and infect us. What is that music? That African barbarism!

Creux exits with his gun.

DOÑA SMERALDA (*dancing seductively*) Do you know this new dance? *"Dansez Bamboula! Bad-oum!"*

DOÑA POLISSENA *"Bad-doum-bad-DOUM!"* Who is your teacher?

DOÑA SMERALDA I go to Congo Square where all the slaves meet— *"Ba-doum"*

DOÑA POLISSENA (*trying to feel the rhythm*) *"Bad-oum Bad-oum!"* Your husband doesn't mind?

DOÑA SMERALDA I'll give you a list of the things my husband doesn't know!

DOÑA POLISSENA (*trying to find the rhythm*)   Paradise!

DOÑA SMERALDA   *Ba-doum!*

DOÑA POLISSENA   My body has never moved this way—*Ba-doum*

DOÑA SMERALDA   It will in New Orleans.

Gunshots. Creux returns, followed by ORPHEE.

ORPHEE (*to Doña Smeralda*)   Your honored guest shot at us!

DOÑA SMERALDA   You mustn't shoot our slaves!

CREUX   I won't miss the next time. The odor of pomade on his black half-kinked hair sickens me.

Orphee barks.

CREUX   Don't be frightened, dear.

Orphee exits, laughing.

CREUX   *Sante Domingue?* A perfect civilization distorted by those leprous words of *liberte, fraternite, egalite,* which have no right in the mouth of the Negro.

DOÑA POLISSENA   It is the voice of history. This is a time of revolution.

CREUX   I curse all revolution. The Americans, the French gave too many people the idea of freedom.

DOÑA POLISSENA   What else could they have done?

CREUX   Had their revolutions, but done them in secret!

Jacques enters the garden. Murmur follows.

JACQUES CORNET   Stay at hand.

DR. T   As Jacques Cornet enters, let me take you to Paris.

Napoleon sits in a bathtub. Tallyrand paces studying a map of the world. Josephine does tarot cards.

NAPOLEON   I have lost the Rhine.

TALLYRAND   That is a sign from our creator to change directions. Oh Most Blessed Angel of Military Brilliance, move from Europe to the New World! The source of infinite wealth!

Tallyrand reveals a map of the vast Louisiana Territory.

NAPOLEON   Spain would never give us all this.

TALLYRAND (*waving a letter*)   It will now. *Carlos Cuarto*—an utter jackass—wants something from us.

CARLOS CUARTO, *King of Spain, and his daughter, the* INFANTA, *appear. She has one eye and eats greedily.*

CARLOS CUARTO   Illustrious First Consul, I who am as great a power as has ever existed in the history of the world except for you, come bowing to the might of France. My daughter has found a husband and would like to be a queen. We don't need a large kingdom. She only has one eye.

INFANTA   I'd like my husband to be King of—Tuscany!

TALLYRAND   Tuscany is now called Etruria.

INFANTA   I want Etruria.

NAPOLEON   In exchange for what?

CARLOS CUARTO   Spain has nothing! Our colonies bleed us dry.

TALLYRAND   They are parasites, these colonies. Let us take a colony off your hands. We will give your son-in-law the throne of Etruria in exchange for—where? Here? Here? Here? No—Louisiana.

Tallyrand reveals the map of the Louisiana Territory.

28

JOSEPHINE (*whispering*) Not Louisiana! The Indies! I want my muslins washed!

TALLYRAND (*whispering*) Believe me, you want Louisiana.

JOSEPHINE (*whispering*) Whom do you listen to? Talleyrand or me?

NAPOLEON (*whispering*) I'm trying to take a bath.

JOSEPHINE (*whispering*) Your itch. Always your itch!

NAPOLEON Get Louisiana! Let me take my fucking bath.

Napoleon exits.

JOSEPHINE Don't take Louisiana! Are you insane! Money! Get money!

Josephine follows.

CARLOS CURATO But France gave Louisiana to us thirty-seven years ago.

TALLYRAND We apologize for foisting it off on you. A colony is like having a spoiled *Infanta* for a child.

INFANTA Don't let him talk like that to me!

TALLYRAND Present *Infantas* excluded.

CARLOS CUARTO America *is* a nuisance. I don't even believe these tales of volcanoes that spew gold.

TALLYRAND You've dissuaded me. We don't want Louisiana. Goodbye.

INFANTA No! I'll kill myself and then I'll die and you'll be sorry.

She gorges her mouth with grapes and chokes. Carlos Cuarto performs Heimlich.

CARLOS CUARTO (*to Talleyrand*)   *Carissima!* You want Louisiana? Take Louisiana. New Orleans is no Havana.

TALLYRAND   Oh, all right. Sign this treaty.

Talleyrand produces a paper. Carlos Cuarto signs. The Infanta smiles.

TALLEYRAND (*bowing to the Infanta*)   The Queen of Etruria. And let us keep this treaty a secret until Napoleon is safely across the Atlantic and in view of New Orleans.

They go.

DR. T (*to us*)   You now know more than the majority of people in this play.

Jacques Cornet takes out a key and enters Doña Smeralda's bedroom. He lies on her bed. Jacques Cornet whistles an elaborate whistle. Think of a nightingale in heat. Doña Smeralda stands.

CREUX   Had their revolutions, but done them in secret!

DOÑA SMERALDA (*beaming with joy*)   I don't feel well!

MORALES   Bayou fever?

DOÑA SMERALDA   A definite fever.

She goes into the bedroom and embraces Jacques Cornet.

PINCEPOUSSE   What bird makes that call?

MORALES   It's odd. I hear it all the time.

Jacques Cornet begins undressing her, then himself.

JACQUES CORNET   Have they found the cipher breaker?

DOÑA SMERALDA   Haven't you come to see me?

JACQUES CORNET   *Only you.*

PINCEPOUSSE   Look in there!

MORALES   The door is locked! Dearest, may I come in?

DOÑA SMERALDA (*calling*)   No, adored one! I don't want you catching what I have.

DOÑA POLISSENA (*knocking*)   Is it yellow fever?

DOÑA SMERALDA (*calling*)   It's a fever of a different color.

Jacques Cornet embraces her.

MORALES (*calls*)   Dearest Orgasm of My Eyeballs, could my Imperial code breaker be in our temple of joy?

DOÑA SMERALDA (*calling*)   What does it look like?

MORALES   A long black tube with a red ribbon on it.

DOÑA SMERALDA (*calling*)   It sounds familiar. I'll keep my eyes open.

MORALES   Will you be well enough to go to Senor Coquet's ball?

DOÑA POLISSENA (*calling*)   Say you will go! I yearn to dance. *Ba-doum!*

CREUX   No African dancing!

MORALES   Shall I call *Docteur* Toubib?

DOÑA SMERALDA (*calling*)   I know exactly what he'll say. Stay in bed till tomorrow.

JACQUES CORNET (*to us*)   A seduction doesn't count unless it's taking place under the husband's nose.

MORALES   The poor thing relies on me for everything.

JACQUES CORNET   Where is the cipher breaker?

DOÑA SMERALDA (*whisper*)   What is this cipher? I am a code who needs to be broken.

JACQUES CORNET   Of course. (*He turns down the lamp.*) (*to us*) Let me solve this puzzle first. (*He dims the bedroom light.*)

DOÑA SMERALDA (*orgasmic*)   Yes! Yes! Yes!

MORALES   Hear it in her voice? She's getting better.

Enter Margery Jolicoeur.

MARGERY   Where are the best fields to walk in New Orleans?

CREUX (*lunging at her*)   Get thee behind me, Negress!

MORALES   She is our house guest!

CREUX   In which house?

MORALES   In this house.

CREUX (*to Margery*)   I know what you're up to.

MARGERY   I just want to take a walk.

PINCEPOUSSE   Margery! Get upstairs!

MARGERY   I just want to see New Orleans!

Jacques Cornet, curious, peers out through the door.

JACQUES CORNET   Ahh, the lovely woman Pincepousse calls a man.

Doña Smerelda pulls him back to bed.

CREUX   You evil black voodoo witch!

PINCEPOUSSE (*restraining Margery*)   She is my wife—

MARGERY (*as they go*)   I could have had more fun in Natchez and Natchez is no fun.

Pincepousse drags her off.

CREUX   Wife! We're leaving.

POLISSENA   To go where? We're homeless.

MORALES   Leda!!

LEDA *appears. Creux shrieks.*

CREUX   Another wife?

MORALES   Our slave.

PINCEPOUSSE   Leda, go to the guest room and costume her as a boy. An ugly boy.

MORALES   Leda's perfectly happy here, aren't you? For without the blessing of slavery, she wouldn't be a Christian.

LEDA (*to us*)   If I had an axe, I'd chop their heads off.

Leda smiles and goes.

CREUX   We will go to the ball as corpses. I shall costume myself as a ghost of what the white man used to be.

DOÑA POLISSENA   Your wife looked a sweet thing.

JACQUES CORNET (*sizing up Doña Polissena*)   As you look a bit of succulence. Who is she?

Doña Smerelda pulls him back to the bed.

CREUX   Sweet? She'd slash our throats and then lick the knife. I am shocked by the laxity of morals I see in New Orleans.

MORALES   We thought if we gave the Negro some freedoms, he would be less likely to revolt.

CREUX   You've gone too far. Spain must come to her senses and restore *le Code Noir.*

Jacques Cornet interrupts the scene and comes down to us, wrapping his cloak around him.

JACQUES CORNET (*to us*)   Let me tell you about this thing called *le Code Noir,* promulgated by the so-called Sun King in the year 1685. A Royal Edict Touching on the State and Discipline of the Black Slaves of Louisiana, Given at Versailles in the Month of March. We have judged that it was a matter of our authority and our justice, for the conservation of this colony, to establish there a law concerning the discipline of slaves. No slaves may marry without permission of their master. No slave can sell anything without written permission of his master. Slaves of different masters who congregate in a group shall be whipped and then branded with a *fleur de lys*. No slaves may bear arms or large sticks. Children born of slaves belong to the master of the mother. A slave who strikes his master shall be put to death. Slaves are the master's personal property. Oh, I've memorized every clause, every syllable, every letter of the notorious black code, which gave no rights to blacks, declaring them mere pieces of property.

This stellar document shone forth from the sacred light of Louis XIV—the Sun King. What kind of sun shines this hatred? The sun that God created was made to nourish and insure life's growth, a light as gold as a lion's mane. But *le Code Noir*? The sun of this Sun King only shrivels and dries, is a sun that never rises, a sun with no dawn—a blazing sun that puts ice around your eyelids, a burning sun that gives no heat but is up there an arctic block of ice at the heart of the universe— that sun to me is dark and silent as the moon. The sun of this Sun King is a pus-filled canker of hate, a rotting cancer, a phaeton's chariot spewing out rot at its highest point of ascent.

But that's all in the past. No, we now are on fire in this Age of Enlightenment—the way a magnifying glass catches the sun's blaze and sets paper into flame—so the free and full splendoured sun shines in our day of universal *liberte, egalite, fraternite*. The French Revolution and the American Revolution brought the nurturing heat back to the sun, revived the sun. We stand in its heat. *Le Code Noir est mort.* We can never return to those principles that were so easily strewn in the gutter years of *Louis Quatorze*—even to say it *quatorze quatorze*—like the croak of a cancerous frog—no, the head of Louis XVI, his heir, rolled into the straw basket under the guillotine along with the foolish scepter that issued such proclamations. *Le Code Noir* is dead. This is the Age of Enlightenment. (*Jacques Cornet bows and returns to bed with Doña Smeralda.*) Ouch! (*He holds up a black tube with a red ribbon on it*) Is this the cipher machine? This is it! Give it to him!

DOÑA SMERALDA Careful!

MORALES Did you say something, Moon of Magnificence?

DOÑA SMERALDA (*calling*) Darlingest, Delight of My Dreams? I think I found it.

MORALES The cipher machine? Let me come in!

DOÑA SMERALDA Don't let him see you.

Jacques opens the door a crack, passes the code breaker out to Morales who kisses Jacques' hand, then slams the door.

MORALES I will now decipher the cryptogram. The code is "Mississippi".

Morales uses the chart of the code breaker as Pincepoussse prepares to take dictation. Letters of the alphabet appear overhead. Then letters beneath the alphabet spell out M.I.S.P., which take the first four slots. M is under A. I is under B. S is under C. P under D. M.I.S.P. becomes the first four letters of the alphabet. The coded alphabet continues. A is E. B is F.

DR. T At the same time, in Washington D.C., spies in France have delivered the same secret message to Mr. Jefferson.

Jefferson enters followed by Meriwether who carries the cipher breaker.

JEFFERSON The key is "Artichoke".

MORALES So A is M.

PINCEPOUSSE B is I.

MORALES C is S.

MERIWETHER   A is F.
   R is A.

JEFFERSON   C is E.

MORALES   D is P.

PINCEPOUSSE   V is R.

JACQUES CORNET   Can you see what they're doing?

JEFFERSON   L is A.

MERIWETHER   P is N.

The letters overhead spin madly until they form a message. "Spain has given Louisiana to France".

DR. T *(to us)*   But you knew that already.

JACQUES CORNET   What does it say! I can't see it!

MORALES   The floor of the world trembles beneath my feet.

DOÑA POLISSENA   Good news?

CREUX   Good news died with the invention of the wheel.

PINCEPOUSSE   I'm having a delusion. I thought you said Spain has given Louisiana to a country now ruled by a Corsican dwarf!

JACQUES CORNET   Did he say Spain has given all of Louisiana to France?

JACQUES CORNET   Go out there! Learn what's in that letter!

DOÑA SMERALDA   He'll be suspicious. I'm not interested in anything.

JEFFERSON   Whatever power other than ourselves holds the country west of the Mississippi becomes our natural enemy. This is an act of war!

Jefferson exits, followed by Meriwether.

MORALES   I shall not be discarded like the skin of a mango! Yes! That day is here!

JACQUES CORNET   What day is here?

MORALES (*whisper*)   Our plan.

PINCEPOUSSE (*whisper*)   What plan?

JACQUES CORNET   What are they saying?

MORALES (*whisper*)   The plan we had talked about pursuing one day.

PINCEPOUSSE (*whisper*)   Which plan?

JACQUES CORNET   I cannot be excluded!

MORALES (*smacking Pincepousse*)   You dunce! Our plan requires money!

Margery appears, dressed as a boy.

MARGERY   Are we going to the ball?

PINCEPOUSSE   Napoleon will want Margery! Napoleon will not have you!

Pincepousse drags Margery off.

MORALES   I have no money. Do you?

CREUX   I have no money!

Pincepousse returns.

PINCEPOUSSE   I have no money.

MORALES   Only Jacques Cornet has money.

CREUX   Finally to meet a good man. Is he on our side?

PINCEPOUSSE   He is a lecher! I loathe him! And there's one other thing—

Jacques Cornet, now dressed, appears at the side of the stage, Murmur at his side.

JACQUES CORNET   Only one?

MORALES   (*to Pincepousse*)   Do not reveal Jacques' racial background to this lunatic until we have Jacques' money. . . . My dear cousin M. Pincepousse and I must attend to the power of my office. Prepare for the ball! I see you in a toga! The two of you will shine tonight!

Creux and Doña Polissena go.

MORALES   Come with me to the *Cabildo*!

DR. T   City Hall.

MORALES   And give Cornet no suspicion of needing money for revolution. He'll attempt to intrude.

PINCEPOUSSE   How will we get money out of him?

JACQUES CORNET   Yes. How will you?

MORALES   What is Jacques' weak point?

JACQUES CORNET   Fashion!

MORALES   Maps! We will create a new map to sell to Jacques Cornet!

JACQUES CORNET   As I have a new map of you, you swine. Murmur, go to the Cabildo. Follow these men. Find out their plans. I am not surrendering one ounce of my authority!

Doña Smerelda, half-dressed, runs to Jacques Cornet.

DOÑA SMERALDA   You love only me?

JACQUES CORNET (*embracing her*)   I love only you. (*to us*)   And you and you.

DOÑA SMERALDA   You'll always protect my honor?

JACQUES CORNET   As I would protect my wardrobe.

He goes.

The street outside Morales' home.

JACQUES CORNET (*to Murmur*)   Any return of *le Code Noir* will surely not apply to me. I control the flow of money in this town. I am safe. Anxiety is a slave's emotion.

MURMUR   Or so he thinks.

Doña Athena appears. Jacques Cornet and Murmur go. Doña Athena follows.

Morales and Pincepousse enter the Cabildo.

MORALES   Has anyone seen us?

PINCEPOUSSE   No one.

MORALES   Revolution makes me thirsty! I need a drink. Slave!

Murmur appears as an old man, carrying a tray of drinks.

MORALES   We will unite North and South America. One nation from Canada to Tierra del Fuego, ruled by me, no longer *Supreme,* but elevated to *Glorioso Intendante.* I am no longer El Cid. I am Jorge Washington of *Nova Spania.*

PINCEPOUSSE   And I?

MORALES   You are vice-*Glorioso Intendante.* We must raise a militia.

PINCEPOUSSE   Margery will love me then. (*seeing Murmur*) Who is he?

MURMUR   I's jest cleanin' up.

MORALES   There's a dustball in that corner.

PINCEPOUSSE   Can he understand?

MURMUR   I never hears nothin'. The way everything is suits me fine.

MORALES   I will restore to you all that Jacques Cornet has wrongfully taken from you.

PINCEPOUSSE   My house? My money? Everything my father left him?

MORALES   Everything! And Margery shall be our queen!

PINCEPOUSSE   To *Nova Spania!*

They go. Murmur runs to Jacques Cornet with the news.

JACQUES CORNET   *Nova Spania?* Surely if there's a new nation, I must hold a high rank in it. But wait! The Frenchman? The Englishman? Have they received their own coded message? Murmur, the keys.

DOÑA ATHENE *appears. Jacques Cornet sees her and flees.*

DOÑA ATHENE   Was not the world a vast prison, and women born slaves? Come back. Come back!

Doña Athene pursues Murmur and Jacques Cornet.

The docks. Margery appears, dressed as a boy.

MARGERY (*to us*)   I love this free port—walking along the docks and piers, seeing ships from all over the world depositing their goods. I hear every language known to man. I just met an Egyptian. I love the colors of all the skin that I see. The browns, the blacks, the yellows, the pinks, the white, quadroons, mulattoes, samboes, mestizos, Indians, and other commixtures not yet classified. Listen! Hear bagpipes on one ship and Italian mandolins on another. Breathe! The scent of the food. No city on this planet can be more varied, more

motley, more multifarious. Is there another place where no
barriers exist between people? A world where people join,
meet, all equals. Oh, there are slaves but if you're a slave you
can work to buy your freedom because the more people
that are free, the better we all will be. If the presence of
Pincepousse is the price I must pay for being in this paradise,
I'll pay! Perfection.

Pincepousse appears. She sees him and flees.

*Mardi Gras! New Orleans is a riot of drumming and dancing and lots
of badoum. Floats! Carnival! Joy!*

Jacques Cornet appears, making his way through the ecstatic throng.

JACQUES CORNET   As a bee invades its body into combs,
    so must I now penetrate their homes.
    The home of the Yankee Sparks.

Jacques whistles that whistle. MRS. SPARKS *appears behind a
wrought iron gate.*

MRS. SPARKS   Oh Jacques, it's not the right time.

JACQUES CORNET   Oh Blessed damozel, with you I always
    know the time. I think of you, the clock within my body
    sweeps to high noon.

MRS. SPARKS   But my husband is home.

JACQUES CORNET   Is he my rival?

MRS. SPARKS   Never. Mr. Sparks just says trifling things like
    Barbary pirates declared war on the United States.

JACQUES CORNET   War? Why would your husband know this?

MRS. SPARKS   Mr. Sparks relays information to the State
    Department for the new president.

JACQUES CORNET   The United States has a new president?
    What happened to the old one?

MRS. SPARKS We elect a new one every four years.

JACQUES CORNET What a ridiculous system. This new
president will need a man to oversee deliveries to the port of
New Orleans. Could your husband get a message to—

Sparks enters. Mrs. Sparks retreats.

SPARKS Cornet! What brings you here?

JACQUES CORNET Oh. What's new on the Rialto?

SPARKS Is anything ever truly new?

JACQUES CORNET Sometimes the world wears a new cloak?

SPARKS Is everything fashion with you?

JACQUES CORNET Well, yes.

MRS. SPARKS *(appearing)* Who is this man, dear?

SPARKS No one. *(to us)* Cornet is trying to get into my
house for a spot of fornication with my wife.—Sorry,
Cornet. We're off to the ball. Then I forego all social calls for
Lent.

Mr. and Mrs. Sparks go. Mardi Gras swirls around him.

JACQUES CORNET I freed him from his debt. How dare he
disregard me? But what does Great Britain know? The home
of Lord and Lady Harcourt.

*Jacques Cornet whistles that whistle. LADY HARCOURT appears
behind a wrought iron gate.*

LADY HARCOURT Jacques! It's been days!

JACQUES CORNET But now I'm here. I've come to clasp you
naked in my longing arms, to taste your nimble tongue—
We'll explore all nooks and crannies
with a detour to our fannies.

LADY HARCOURT   I'm free! With the news my husband got today he won't notice I'm away.

JACQUES CORNET   What news?

LADY HARCOURT   I was shocked. Aghast.
    It seems that France—the plan is vast!

JACQUES CORNET   Why would your husband have privileged information?

LADY HARCOURT   My husband spies for the crown. Can we meet after the ball?

JACQUES CORNET (*to us*)   Harcourt spies for England? I can work with England. I'm more British than they. Could your husband send a message from me to the king?

Lord Harcourt appears. Lady Harcourt goes.

HARCOURT   You? Pay a social call?

JACQUES CORNET   Harcourt! It was an enchantment seeing you earlier today. Hypothetical question. What would England do if, say, Napoleon took, say, Louisiana away from, say, Spain?

HARCOURT   Spain give up this paradise? I don't think you need worry your bewigged little perfumed head about that. I'd ask you in but my wife is very ugly.

JACQUES CORNET   Harcourt! Could we meet man to man?

HARCOURT (*to us*)   He just wants my wife.—Meet man to man? No!

Lord Harcourt goes. Jacques Cornet goes through the merrymakers looking for the men who were at his house earlier. Dorilante, Pythagore, Sparks, Harcourt, Alcibiade, appear, ignoring him.

JACQUES CORNET   Dorliante, it's me! Alcibiade! I just need one moment. Just one minute. Just one moment. Just one minute.

THE MEN   So sorry. Must run. So sorry. Can't stop. So sorry. Godbye.

They shun him and go.

JACQUES CORNET   You think I want your wives? I've had your wives. You knot of mouth-friends! Henceforth, hated be! These men once groveled at my feet. A coded message arrives. They suddenly hold back. I need to play a role in this Hobbesian juggernaut called history. I need to know where I fit?

Jacques Cornet's bedroom. Murmur and Dr. T appear.

JACQUES CORNET   Why won't the men of this town answer my friendship?

DR. T   For starters, you don't look the same as they do.

JACQUES CORNET   I should hope not.

DR. T   Look at your clothes.

MURMUR   Look at theirs. You're the only parade in town.

JACQUES CORNET   A good parade pleases everyone.

DR. T   Not your kind of parade, brazenly trampling every bystander. If you want acceptance, purge yourself of all outward signs of foppery. The man of the nineteenth century no longer stands out. He dresses in black.

JACQUES CORNET   The color of Satan?

DR. T (*snatching off Jacques's peruke*)   And men now show their scalps.

JACQUES CORNET (*putting the wig back on his head*)   Have men no modesty? Give this up? I'd as soon forfeit an arm or a leg or—

MURMUR   Or what?

JACQUES CORNET   The only scepter I allow to rule me.

DR. T   Now that you mention it. Another motive for men's alarm is that sea monster of yours lurking beneath the waves, waiting to attack their wives.

JACQUES CORNET   What are you talking about?

DR. T   The arm of a five-year-old boy holding out an apple.

MURMUR   Flamingoes flying home and some guy's wife being the nest.

JACQUES CORNET   Apples? Flamingoes?

DR. T   Jacques. Your endowments are legendary.

JACQUES CORNET   That? Don't all men have one?

MURMUR   Every country has a river but not all are the Mississippi.

JACQUES CORNET   I am so alone in the world.

MURMUR   You have us, boss.

JACQUES CORNET   But you have no power. They do. I merely want their faith.

DR. T   Faith? Faith? Look at your wife, your women. You don't know the first thing about faith.

JACQUES CORNET   You err, Dr. T. I never showed more faith then when my father was on his deathbed with his estate unsettled. I sat by his side. I flattered. I cajoled. I echoed his thoughts. His jokes were my jokes. His opinions mine. I became as his mirror. That faith bought me my freedom and my power.

MURMUR   If you named me in your will, I'd be lapping your face.

JACQUES CORNET   Don't you now?

45

MURMUR   Sure—but my teeth wouldn't be gritted.

JACQUES CORNET   Ahh! The idea uncanny! Suppose I were to die and each man thought he were my sole heir?

MURMUR   Die?

JACQUES CORNET   If I unleashed word that I lingered in the neighborhood of death . . . and left a will. Yes! I will make every man in New Orleans think he is my sole heir. Yes! After a jealous husband shot me for seducing his wife and left me in the gutter like an empty champagne bottle. I'm about to hover in the shady land between life and death. (*He pulls out pen and paper*)   My last will and testament: Being of sound mind but not of body, I leave all my worldly goods to . . . ta ta tah—ta ta ah! Fill in the names of Morales—Harcourt— Dorilante—Sparks. Find each man in private. Tell him not to share word of this largesse with any other man.

DR. T   You've gone mad.

JACQUES CORNET   I've gone sane! I will rid myself of everything that puts a space between me and them. The name of my play is now *A Free Man of Color or the Things We Do for Power.*

Napoleon in military splendor appears, followed by Tallyrand.

TALLYRAND   The luck of Napoleon. The slave rebellion in *Sante Domingue* is there for your cover. You will sail your ships to the Indies merely to put down this tiresome rebellion. Mission accomplished in a few days. You sail up the Caribbean into the Gulf of Mexico. Possess New Orleans, the mouth of the Mississippi. The birth of *Nouvelle France!*

NAPOLEON   *Napoleona!*

TALLYRAND   The name is immaterial. The money not.

NAPOLEON   I can't leave France now.

TALLYRAND   Then send your brother-in-law to lead the fleet.

DR. T   General le Clerc, known by one and all, behind his back, as the Blond Bonaparte, bounces on.

GENEAL LE CLERC *bounces on.*

LE CLERC   I sail wherever you say, Citizen Consul, except—

NAPOLEON   You hesitate?

LE CLERC   May I tell a secret, which in no way reflects upon my unchallenged manhood? Scorpions. I'm told in the Indies you step out of bed, scorpions wait.

Josephine appears.

JOSEPHINE   In *Martinique,* we placed the legs of the bed in pans of water so the scorpions could not crawl in. Pans of water from bed to toilet to desk. We hopped from pan to pan and quite loved the exercise. Pans of water and you're safe.

LE CLERC   Hop? Hop? Hop? The West Indies will be such fun.

The French contingent goes. Enter Jefferson and Meriwether.

JEFFERSON   Instruct Robert Livingston to get here! I'm sending him to France at once!

Meriwether brings on LIVINGSTON, *who listens through an ear trumpet.*

DR. T   Robert Livingston appears. The scion of one of the richest, oldest families in the United States.

LIVINGSTON   Go where?

JEFFERSON   Paris?

LIVINGSTON   Harris?

JEFFERSON   Paris, France.

LIVINGSTON   I'm Minister to France.

JEFFERSON   I'm appointing you Minister Plenipotentiary!

LIVINGSTON   Put me in a penitentiary?

JEFFERSON   I'm giving you more powers!

LIVINGSTON   Flowers?

JEFFERSON   (*in Livingston's ear trumpet*)   You must stop France from taking New Orleans!

LIVINGSTON   What about New Orleans?

Meriwether wheels in a blackboard with the words FRANCE NOW OWNS NEW ORLEANS *written in large letters.*

LIVINGSTON   France now owns New Orleans! Never!

JEFFERSON   Get New Orleans! I authorize you to spend up to two million dollars.

LIVINGSTON   I don't speak any French.

JEFFERSON   Money is the great translator.

The American contingent goes.

JACQUES CORNET   Murmur, put out word that I have burned my wardrobe. You say men fear me with their wives? Dr. T, you will tell New Orleans that in checking my physique, *post actus reus*, you were shocked to find an absence.

MURMUR   That? You're talking about that?

JACQUES CORNET   Yes. A gunshot has removed the skeleton key that once fit all the locks of Louisiana. Now may I have, by the reputation of a eunuch, the privileges of one; and be trusted with information by the lords of the town. Murmur, bring me my pistol. (*Murmur goes.*)   Doctor T, you'll make the announcement? My conspiracy will need verification.

DR. T   Hippocrates will reach down and slay me.

JACQUES CORNET   Hippocrates will applaud. (*Murmur returns with the pistol.*)   Murmur, do your job.

Murmur cocks the pistol and kneels. Dr. T holds up Jacques Cornet's breeches.

JACQUES CORNET (*cont.*)   Farewell, all senseless thoughts of remorse.
I would remove what e'er would stop my course.

Murmur shoots between the legs.

JACQUES CORNET (*cont.*)   Oh, Murmur, say that the brigand took two shots.

Murmur shoots again. Dr. T holds up the silk breeches marred by two bullet wounds at the groin. Jacques Cornet is very pleased.

JACQUES CORNET (*cont.*)   I am as that fiery star the sun.
I decree what plants will grow or not.
No man uproots me and plants me in *his* pot!
Born to myself, I like myself alone.
Murmur, bring my *flaçon* of *eau de cologne.*

The Haydn plays. Jacques Cornet, Murmur and Dr. T bow to us. Murmur draws the curtain closed.

ACT ONE CURTAIN

ACT TWO

The Ball. Music and dancing. The gun shot. Everyone stops. Then they resume dancing. The second gun shot. A moment of alarm. Then everyone returns to the spirit of the ball. Margery enters, costumed as a boy and carrying a mask.

MARGERY (*to us*)   What a world of fine folks here is. But I don't see the gentleman that loves me. I have got the Louisiana disease they call love. When I think of my husband, I have the inclination to vomit, but when I think of my dear mystery man, my hot fever comes, and I am in a fever indeed and need to be where he is. Oh sick sick. Where? There!

Margery throws herself at a masked man. It's Pincepousse.

PINCEPOUSSE   You'll not dance with any man. Tonight *you're* a man.

MARGERY   I'll yet find the man who owns my soul.

Dr. T enters, carrying Jacques' shot-up breeches.

DR. T (*quiet, to Morales*)   Someone has shot Jacques Cornet.

MORALES   Is he dead?

DR. T   In a manner of speaking.

MORALES (*shock, then glee*)   Tell it to me again.

DR. T   And I trust you to tell no one this humiliating event.

MORALES   No one. My oath.

DR. T   Naturally, the news travels.

Morales runs to Pincepousse and whispers.

PINCEPOUSSE   Thank God!

HARCOURT   I have an alibi!

ALCIBIADE   I better have an alibi!

PINCEPOUSSE   I don't want an alibi.

CREUX   Is no man safe in New Orleans?

DOÑA POLISSENA   You're safe, dear. You're safe.

DOÑA SMERELDA   God cannot be so cruel!

MRS. SPARKS   My joy is amputated!

LADY HARCOURT   I am buried alive!

DOÑA SMERALDA   Suicide!

MME DORILANTE   My life is over!

DOÑA SMERALDA (*to Dr. T*)   There's nothing you can do?

DR. T (*showing her the breeches*)   The pistol's aim was impeccable.

Doña Smeralda is inconsolable.

MORALES   Another jereboam of champagne!

THE MEN   Let's toast!

ALCIBIADE   Let's raise a statue to the man who did it.

PYTHAGORE   No! Raise a statue to Cornet.

HARCOURT   Will it be before or after his loss?

PYTHAGORE   After! A great wind will blow through its lower portions!

HARCOURT   Has he truly become a *berdache*?

SPARKS   A what?

HARCOURT   A *berdache* is a North American Indian transvestite. Let's call Jacques *Berdache*!

DORILANTE   *Berdache! Berdache!*

MORALES (*to Pincepousse*)   *Nova Spania* lives! Get Jacques'
money before it's too late.

PINCEPOUSSE (*nodding*)   Where is Margery? Margery!

*Pincepousse finds Margery and drags her out. Murmur enters, carrying
a number of wills.*

DR. T   Murmur arrives. He takes each of the husbands aside.

MURMUR (*to each, separately distributing the wills*)   Supreme
Intendante.
   Mr. Sparks.
   Monsieur Dorilante.
   Harcourt.
   Read the final wishes from the pen of a dying man.

MORALES (*reads*)   A last will and testament? Good god!

DORILANTE (*reads*)   I am his sole heir!

SPARKS (*reads*)   He leaves me everything?

HARCOURT (*reads*)   His fortune comes to me?

MURMUR   The wax is warm yet and the ink scarce dry upon
the parchment.

SPARKS   By what good chance, sweet Murmur?

DORILANTE   Why would heaven befriend me?

HARCOURT   Are you sure?

MURMUR   Your dessert, sir; I know no second cause.
   I oft have heard Jacques say, how he admired
   You.
   You.
   You.
   You.
   So wise, so grave; when every word
   your worship but lets fall, is a pearl of great price.

MORALES 'Tis true.

SPARKS He sees me as I am.

DORILANTE I loved the man!

HARCOURT How much money does Jacques Cornet have?

MURMUR Enough to sink a sloop.

HARCOURT Or let one sail. How can I be of service while he lives?

DORILANTE How may I show my gratitude before death snatches him away?

SPARKS —let the man know I loved him?

MORALES —give comfort in his last hours?

MURMUR My master has heard of *Nova Spania* and would like to play a part in it—if he lives.

MORALES How did he know about *Nova Spania?*

MURMUR His half-brother?

MORALES Of course! That dolt. I must not let Pincepousse know I am the sole heir to Jacques Cornet. Tell Jacques he won't miss the love business. Very overrated.

MURMUR (*to Sparks*) All my dying master wants in return is to become a friend of Thomas Jefferson! Supreme Councilor of Democracy!

SPARKS A goodly title if posthumous. I shall arrange that.

HARCOURT (*to Murmur*) Tell your master King George would be proud to count him as an ally and give him an honor. Knight of the Silver Stick? Yes, I love it.

MURMUR And tell no other man this news.

MORALES No one.

SPARKS   No one.

HARCOURT   No one.

DORILANTE   No one. Jacques Cornet

HARCOURT   shall be an integral part

SPARKS   of the future of

MORALES/SPARKS/DORILANTE/HARCOURT   New Orleans!

SPARKS   Look! What's that fire!

DORILANTE   Murmur, a fire rages outside your master's window!

MURMUR   No worry. My master is simply burning his entire wardrobe and dressing in black. His last words to me were "oh men of New Orleans, how beautiful to dress as they do!"

HARCOURT   I knew he'd come to his senses.

THE MEN   *Berdache! Berdache!*

The men cackle triumphantly and go.

Jacques Cornet's bedroom, filled with flowers. Jacques Cornet, Murmur, and Dr. T enter, laughing.

JACQUES CORNET   Isn't it the most wondrous fun? Do tell me again Murmur, and pour that champagne.

MURMUR   (*as they drink*)   Morales said this love business is overrated.

JACQUES CORNET   At least by the impotent.

MURMUR   And look at the flowers you've received! "From your best friend."

DR. T   "I have written to Napoleon"

MURMUR   "To the people of *Nova Spania*"

54

DR. T "To Jefferson"

MURMUR "From one who adores you"

JACQUES CORNET Are these from the wives or the husbands?

A sudden knock at the door, alarming Jacques Cornet and Dr. T.

MURMUR I have told everyone you may receive no visitors. (*to the door*) Whom that?

Pincepousse appears in the antechamber with a cranky Margery.

PINCEPOUSSE (*to Murmur*) I wish to talk to my brother and reconcile with him before he dies. I know he's in there!

Jacques Cornet and Dr. T burst into laughter.

DR. T Get into bed! Remember the part you have chosen. I must go now and make my reports.

JACQUES CORNET What state am I in?

DR. T Feverish.

JACQUES CORNET (*getting into bed*) I can do that.

Dr. T goes into the antechamber.

PINCEPOUSSE Doctor Toutou, are you going to prepare the funeral?

DR. T He's hanging on by a silken thread.

MARGERY I don't want to see any man who's had his whoosiz shot off.

PINCEPOUSSE You wait outside!

MARGERY I don't want to wait outside!

PINCEPOUSSE What will I do with her?

DR. T Take her in with you. Every man in New Orleans is safe.

JACQUES CORNET My half-brother is the only man who offers me nothing. But his country wife is another matter.

Pincepousse and Margery come quietly into the "sick" room.

JACQUES CORNET *(cont.)* *(in a daze)* Dies iræ, dies illa, dies calamitatis et miseriæ.

Murmur swings incense and joins in the dirge in a jazzy riff. Murmur exits as Pincepousse goes to Jacques Cornet's bedside.

PINCEPOUSSE I hate him so I am paralyzed. First of all, let me be brief. The subject is money.

JACQUES CORNET You're giving me money? How dear.

PINCEPOUSSE No!

MARGERY *(to us)* But that's the man for who it is I search! He's the one the bullet found? My luck to find my dream the day he lost *his* luck.

JACQUES CORNET Prithee, who is this pretty young gentleman? Come closer.

PINCEPOUSSE Don't move! I possess a most magnificent map that will reveal the passage to the west—But it comes at a price.

JACQUES CORNET No more maps. I'm staying home and doing needlepoint. *(to Margery)* Are you the wife forced to wear your brother's clothes or are you the brother forced to wear your sister's? What a complicated family life you lead. Come closer.

PINCEPOUSSE Go to him. Don't dilly-dally. Tell him you want money.

Margery reluctantly goes to his bedside.

MARGERY *(by rote)* I'm very sorry for the event what has befallen—

Jacques puts her hand under the sheets.

MARGERY (*after a moment*)   Oh! 'tis like being at sea for many days and you're sure there's nothing there until one day a sailor in the crow's nest cries out "Land Ho!" Land Ho!!

JACQUES CORNET   Since I'd never kiss a lad, would you give the bride your sister this humble kiss from me?

PINCEPOUSSE   Hurry—get it over with—Now about the money for the map—(*Margery kisses Jacques over and over. Jacques returns the favor.*)   May ten thousand ulcers gnaw away their lips! How she gazes on him! (*pulls her away*) (*to Jacques*) Sir, I need money—

JACQUES CORNET   Methinks he is so handsome he should not be a man. Are you sure you're a man?

PINCEPOUSSE (*twisting her arm*)   Tell him you're a man. Say it! say it!

MARGERY   I am no woman. (*whispers*)   I am! I am!

JACQUES CORNET   And tell your husband I am no man.

MARGERY   He's not. He's not.—You are! You are!

PINCEPOUSSE   Brother to brother, will you give me the money?

JACQUES CORNET   Have you heard word of Napoleon and New Orleans?

PINCEPOUSSE   What a ridiculous thought.

JACQUES CORNET   Liar. His wife will tell me what he knows.—Murmur, as Cain said to Abel, get me my bag of walking around money. (*Murmur goes*)   Too many visitors. I need air. Pray leave me your wife's brother whilst Murmur gets your gold?

PINCEPOUSSE   Be a good boy!

Pincepousse runs out. Margery jumps into bed.

MARGERY   They told me you were beautiful but they didn't tell me you were this beautiful.

They go under the covers. Dr. T appears.

DR. T   Meanwhile, Livingston in Paris has a much harder time trying to meet Napoleon.

Enter Livingston.

LIVINGSTON   Has Spain given you Louisiana?

Talleyrand appears.

TALLYRAND   I hope such lavish rumors haven't sent you across the sea?

LIVINGSTON   —Liar.

TALLYRAND   Your French is execrable.

Exit Talleyrand.

LIVINGSTON   I will not leave this spot till I speak to Napoleon!

Livingston goes. Enter Jefferson, Meriwether, Toussaint, and Le Clerc.

DR. T   At the same time, Washington, D.C., and Santo Domingo both find themselves in turmoil.

MERIWETHER   Sir! Napoleon's fleet has anchored at the eastern end of Santo Domingo.

TOUSSAINT   I've never seen so large a fleet before.

LE CLERC   We arrive. We wait. We prepare.

MERIWETHER (*over Le Clerc's lines*)   Le Clerc's forces amount to sixty ships and more than thirty thousand men.

TOUSSAINT   Why are they here?

MERIWETHER   Is this war?

LECLERC   We arrive. We wait. We prepare.
We arrive. We wait. We prepare

TOUSSAINT   It cannot be war.

JEFFERSON   Not yet.

TOUSSAINT   Yet all France has come to Sante Domingue.

LE CLERC   We arrive. We wait. We prepare.
We arrive. We wait. We prepare.
We arrive. We wait. We prepare.

JEFFERSON   Have we sent the ships bearing food and
ammunition to the Negroes of Santo Domingo?

MERIWETHER   They are in mid-voyage.

LE CLERC   We attack Sante Domingue by land and by sea!
Everything yields to French valor.

TOUSSAINT   France has deceived us. She comes to take revenge
and enslave the blacks. We will not perish! Set the city of
Fort Dauphin afire!

LE CLERC   At the sight of the flames, we slaughter as many
Negroes as we capture, treating them all as revolters.

TOUSSAINT   The bay of *Mancenille* is stained with the blood of
unarmed blacks. We raise an ocean of flame and tease the tide
of fire to Port au Prince. The United States has promised to
send us ammunition and food! We will triumph! Victory or
death for freedom!

Exit Toussaint.

LE CLERC   A scorpion! Put down pans of water. I walk from
pan to pan.

Le Clerc goes. Jacques' bedroom.

MARGERY   Do it again!

JACQUES CORNET   This will be our little secret.

MARGERY   It's an enormous secret!

JACQUES CORNET   Tell me what Pincepousse is up to? What have you heard about this new Spain?

MARGERY   Huh?

JACQUES   What does he talk to you about?

MARGERY   Nothin'! I am with you forever and ever, never to leave your side. Again!

JACQUES CORNET   You know nothing?

MARGERY   One thing! That I love you.

JACQUES CORNET   It's been lovely to meet you. Let Murmur show you the door. Murmur?

MARGERY   I'm not leaving! I'm never going back to Pincepousse again.

Pincepousse enters and sees Margery, half dressed.

PINCEPOUSSE   You. Him. It. Bed.(*rubbing his forehead*)   We're not staying here. Margery means more to me. I take my beloved back home to my plantation. I leave the plot of this play. Goodbye. Say goodbye.

JACQUES CORNET   Adieu.

MARGERY   No! I'm not leaving. No!

Pincepousse drags Margery off.

Toussaint enters.

TOUSSAINT   I search the horizon! I look for ships of salvation! Yes! America will honor our request!

Jefferson and Meriwether enter.

MERIWETHER I can't believe what you're saying—

JEFFERSON Stop the delivery of supplies to Santo Domingo.

MERIWETHER You can't renege on a promise to feed and arm Santo Domingo!

JEFFERSON Order the ships to return to their American port.

MERIWETHER I refuse.

JEFFERSON Do it. We can't allow the cannibal government of Santo Domingo to offend glorious France.

MERIWETHER But you said Toussaint's a legitimate government.

JEFFERSON We don't offend France, not when we want New Orleans. We *must* have New Orleans. Exercise some pragmatism. Order our ships to return.

MERIWETHER But sir, you're an example to the world.

JEFFERSON Thank you, Meriwether. I treasure your support. Now for some lunch. Fanny? Is the ice cream ready? I am starving.

Exit Jefferson.

MERIWETHER But sir, you said—Please release me from these duties.

Meriwether goes.

TOUSSAINT Why are the American ships turning back? No! Mr Jefferson! Your promise! From the head of one government to another, I implore you—Rise up, Lord God! Raise your arm! Do not forget us. My people are starving.

Toussaint goes.

Jacques Cornet's bedroom. Dr. T appears. Jacques is in bed.

JACQUES CORNET   Lent is finally over. How long must I stay on my deathbed?

DR. T (*to us*)   As Santo Domingo burns and Jefferson breaks promises, Jacques Cornet lies in agony in his former bed of pleasure.

JACQUES CORNET   It's been forty days since I last worshipped at the altar of my chosen god?

DR. T   You must be patient. Your God will understand your neglect.

JACQUES CORNET   But not my martyrdom. It's Easter Sunday. One quick holiday visit to the girls of Madame Mandragola?

DR. T   No! Their gossip would burst the mask of your pretence.

JACQUES CORNET   I am bursting!

DR. T   Then travel to another continent to burst.

JACQUES CORNET   May I get some air?

DR. T   Only in heavy disguise. And avoid all your heirs. Happy Easter.

JACQUES   Murmur!

Murmur appears. Jacques and Murmur go out into the town.

MURMUR   The coast is clear, boss.

JACQUES CORNET   A day of beauty. Smell the air. It contains a woman.

Jacques, looking in a window, sees Doña Polissena peering through her microscope.

DOÑA POLISSENA   Dieu! Thou fluttering thing.

JACQUES CORNET   Behold the morsel with the microscope.

DOÑA POLISSENA   So now, I've fixed it.

JACQUES CORNET   Perhaps I might insure her silence.

MURMUR   Boss, don't play with fire.

JACQUES CORNET   Stand guard.

Jacques Cornet enters her laboratory as Doña Polissena puts an insect under her microscope.

JACQUES CORNET   Allow me to introduce myself to you? Jacques Cornet, New Orleans.

DOÑA POLISSSENA   You've recovered from your death?—I'm not interested in a eunuch. One near-eunuch in a household is enough. Excuse me. I find my only solace in science.

JACQUES CORNET (*inhaling her hair*)   May I ask what you're looking for?

DOÑA POLISSENA (*at her microscope*)   The cause of yellow fever. Look—a mosquito was trapped in this letter sent to me from *Sante Domingue*—the *aedes aegypti*—see the female's white markings—(*Jacques Cornet stands behind her, inhaling her hair*) Oh! What are you doing?

JACQUES CORNET   Suddenly, in the presence of you, fair virgin of science, we enter an age of restoration. Lent is over. (*He flings away his cape.*)   Easter morning arrives. He is arisen.

DOÑA POLISSENA   M. Cornet! Come, come here, look through this glass, and see how the blood circulates in the tail of this fish.

JACQUES CORNET (*undoing her shoulder strap*)   But it circulates prettier in this fair neck.

DOÑA POLISSENA (*becoming aroused by his nuzzling of her neck*)   *Ad domos autem ad quotcumque ivero, ibo ad utilitatem eorum.*

JACQUES CORNET   What love potion are you casting?

DOÑA POLISSENA   It is merely the oath of Hippocrates: "Whatever houses I may visit, I will come for the benefit of the sick, and in particular of sexual relations with both female and male persons, be they free or slaves." I find Hippocrates very stimulating to my circulation. *Ba-doum Ba-doum. Ba-doum.*

JACQUES CORNET   (*undoing her shoulder strap*)   You have not loved enough. Your eyes would sparkle and spread. This hand, when touched by him you love, would tremble to your heart. (*He unbuttons her chemise.*)

DOÑA POLISSENA   *Primum non nocere.*

JACQUES CORNET   Yes?

DOÑA POLISSENA   A Latin phrase that means "First, do no harm."

Her dress falls to the ground.

JACQUES CORNET   Tell me more about yellow fever.

Jacques Cornet leads her to her bed. Dr. T appears and draws a curtain around them.

DR. T   Let us draw a curtain as our hero puts Mme. Creux under *his* microscope. Talk of yellow fever makes me think of Santo Domingo.

Napoleon and Le Clerc appear.

NAPOLEON   Is the light from the star of Napoleon to be outshone by a fiery meteor of a Negro? I order you to arrest Toussaint!

LE CLERC   Which we ultimately do.

Toussaint enters in chains.

TOUSSAINT   What bitter irony that hurls my heart to this prison where I must pray to you, the God of the white race,

64

those ferocious tyrants who have always insulted us, you are their God. They took away our gods and forced you on us. To whom else can I now pray? I beg you to destroy their system. As the locusts and boils and plagues that beset Egypt did prove your existence to the chosen people, so the yellow fever makes me believe in you. Because Christ chose the cross, he will love the misery you inflict on the whites.

Toussaint goes. Le Clerc hops from pan to pan of water.

LE CLERC   Three thousand men are dead. We lay corpses out in the barracks yards until they can be carried to lime pits.

NAPOLEON   What is this yellow fever?

GHOSTS *appear.*

VOICES OF SANTO DOMINGO   The disorder begins in the brain accompanied by fever.
Devouring its victim with burning thirst.
Fiery veins streak the eye.
Mucous secretions surcharge the tongue
and take away speech.
When the violence of the disorder approaches the heart,
gums blacken.
Sleep, broken by delirium and convulsions,
yellowish spots spread.
Lips glaze.
Despair paints itself in the eyes.
Sobs form the only language.
The mouth spreads foam
tinged with black and burnt blood.
Death comes on the thirteenth day.

LE CLERC   All remedies are useless.

They go.

Doña Polissena's laboratory.

DOÑA POLISSENA (*from behind the curtained bed*)   Yes! Yes! Yes!

DR. T   And at that moment of carnal delight, Mme. Creux has a blinding revelation.

DOÑA POLISSENA (*opening the bed's curtain*)   The mosquito!

JACQUES CORNET (*appearing over her*)   Excuse me?

DOÑA POLISSENA   The mosquito is the cause of yellow fever! Thank you, Jacques. Give me more scientific insights!

Doña Polissena and Jacques Cornet close the bed's curtain.

DR. T   But no one in science will believe this until October 1900, when Major Walter Reed will announce to the American Public Health Association—

WALTER REED *appears.*

WALTER REED   The mosquito serves as the intermediate host for the parasite of yellow fever.

Tumultuous applause. Walter Reed goes.

Doña Athene appears at the window of the lab peering in at the lovers through a spyglass.

DOÑA ATHENE   His amputation a hoax? I will inform Pincepousse of this deception. I will drag Pincepousse back into the plot of this play. He will be the instrument by which I assassinate my assassin, Jacques Cornet.

Doña Athene goes. Le Clerc enters.

LE CLERC   I saw eight scorpions! I lose 160 men a day. My troops flee to the mountains and find the yellow fever waiting for them. The reinforcements you send die as fast as they arrive. Only 4,500 are fit for duty, bringing our total loss to 29,000 Frenchmen. (*hopping even more slowly from pan to pan*)   Destroy all mountain blacks! Send shiploads of

66

rebellious blacks to American ports. Let New Orleans taste Toussaint's poison! Send these demons out of here!

Le Clerc goes. Ships appear in foggy gloom.

On Mystery Street. Creux enters, Morales following.

CREUX The demons are here! Look on the horizon.

MORALES That ship—

CREUX It comes bearing yellow fever. Yellow fever descends upon New Orleans! We are all in peril.

MORALES We must rescue what we hold most dear.

CREUX I suppose my wife. Although—

MORALES How can we stop them?

CREUX We could flee.

MORALES Never! Find Jacques Cornet and his bottomless purse.

Murmur sees them and calls into Jacques.

MURMUR *(calling in)* Master? Husband alert! Husband alert!

Jacques Cornet and Doña Polissena open the curtain and dress hurriedly.

DOÑA POLISSENA Dear God, I am cursed.

JACQUES CORNET I assume my mask.

Morales and Creux see Murmur.

MORALES Where is Jacques? Jacques! Jacques! Murmur, there you are. Is your master on Mystery Street?

MURMUR Yes. He came to pay a house call on this guy.

CREUX Jacques Cornet is in my house?

MORALES Open up! The nightmare! The infernal French at this moment are vomiting their wretched blacks upon our coast. Jacques! Are you in there?

They enter the laboratory.

CREUX Jacques, I've so hoped to meet you?

Jacques Cornet and Doña Polissena, now presentable, greet Morales and Creux.

JACQUES CORNET Welcome to our sewing circle.

MORALES Santo Domingo arrives in New Orleans! We have to block their entry into the harbor.

CREUX So you're Jacques Cornet. I pray my wife didn't bore you.

MORALES Your clothes? I thought you burned everything.

JACQUES CORNET I'm having your wardrobe duplicated.

CREUX Stop talking about clothes! Tragedy is entering the port.

JACQUES CORNET Tragedy?

CREUX Yellow fever approaches!

DOÑA POLISSENA How thrilling!

MORALES Cornet, as your best friend and sole heir, I implore you. We need salvation.

CREUX *(studying Jacques Cornet)* Is that man a Negro?

MORALES Coz, you have Negroes on the brain! Jacques, only your money can keep New Orleans free of the yellow death. We must pay off the captain and divert the course of disease. New Orleans will call you hero.

MURMUR Don't do it, boss. Please. Stay out of this one!

JACQUES CORNET (*to us*)   Call me hero? The world needs New Orleans. If I were the one to save it, Jefferson, Napoleon, King George—the world!—would be indebted to me! Murmur, bring my gold. Men, to the ship!

Darkness.

DR. T   Fog. Mist. Rain.

They approach the ship by rowboat. The CAPTAIN *appears.*

CAPTAIN   Who goes?

MORALES   Juan Ventura Morales, the *Supreme Intendante* of the Port of New Orleans! State your intentions!

CAPTAIN   We sail by the authority of General Le Clerc!

JACQUES CORNET   We step onboard the ship.

Moans from below.

JACQUES CORNET   What is that moaning?

CREUX   Tell us of the success of General Le Clerc?

Le Clerc appears.

LE CLERC   Most serene First Consul, my leader, my savior. All is going wonderfully. We're making great strides in ridding Sante Domingue of the pestilence of natives, which sets me thinking how much I'd like to return to France. Get me out of hell. You can't imagine the horror—the fever—the smell—the death. I must put down my pen to return to my bed. I just need a rest. Then I shall return to my post. All goes well. We are winning—I—I

Le Clerc dies. He goes.

THE CAPTAIN   Our General is dead! You have to take us in.

MORALES   I engage in business with the captain.

69

Morales and the Captain exit.

JACQUES CORNET   And I ask to see the deported blacks.

MURMUR   Why?

JACQUES CORNET   Curiosity. Open the hold. Open the hold!

Murmur opens the cover of the ship's hold. Doña Polissena, Creux, Jacques Cornet are stunned, repelled by what they see.

MURMUR   We look down into the steerage—

JACQUES CORNET   —into a mass of human agony.

VOICES OF SANTO DOMINGO   *Aidez-moi! Aidez-moi!*

JACQUES CORNET   I see people the color of my mother reaching up—fighting over access to rain—I hear screams.

CREUX   Close the hold! They want to live like this.

POLISENA   It's too horrible.

CREUX   All I hear is how much they want to enjoy the hospitality of New Orleans. They're underprivileged to begin with so this so-called deprivation is working very well for them.

JACQUES CORNET   I see women in labor. A mother lifts her new born infant, her Moses still wet from birth up to me. I reach down . . .

Jacques Cornet falls into the hold. Doña Polissena screams.

MURMUR   My master is down there! I reach my hand down—

Morales returns.

MORALES   Entry denied! Murmur, get us off this ship.

DOÑA POLISSENA   We can't leave Jacques Cornet here!

MORALES Why not! Turn your ship out to sea! We have cannon on shore aimed at you!

Jacques Cornet appears in the hold, a knot of hands clutching at him.

JACQUES CORNET I am a creature with a hundred hands reaching up up up up—

MURMUR The ship is turning—

MORALES Murmur, we must return to our boat.

DOÑA POLISSENA Get him out! Jacques!

MURMUR (*reaching into the hold*) Master! I can't see you! Which hand is yours?

DOÑA POLISSENA (*beating Murmur*) Get him, you fool! Save him!

Jacques Cornet leaps and grabs Murmur's hand.

MURMUR Master! Don't pull me down there! I pull my hand back!

Jacques Cornet struggles.

MORALES I'll not get stuck on this ferry to hell. Drag the cover over the hold.

Murmur catches hold of Jacques Cornet.

JACQUES CORNET I climb up the ladder of flesh. Some rungs of the ladder are still alive—biting me. I stand on top of corpses. I leap!

Jacques Cornet rolls onto the deck, his jacket torn off, his powdered wig gone. Morales slams the cover of the hold shut.

DOÑA POLISSENA You're safe!

MORALES We can't let the fever into our city. Cornet! Into the boat—Murmur, begin rowing!

Murmur rows.

MURMUR (*sings:*)
Row row row your boat
gently down the stream

MORALES We watch the ship of dead men turn away into the
gulf.

The ship leaves the port.

DOÑA POLISSENA Oh, I know that!
(*sings*)
Merrily merrily merrily
life is but a dream

Morales and Creux join in.

JACQUES CORNET (*as they sing*) O miserable mankind, to what
fall
Degraded, to what wretched state reserved!
Who dares his transport vessel cross the waves
with such whose bones are not composed in graves.
The moans of the rejected cling to the fog.
Sight so deform what heart of rock could long
dry-eyed behold? I could not, but weep,
compassion quells and gives me up to tears.

MURMUR/DOÑA POLISSENA/CREUX/MORALES
Merrily merrily merrily
life is but a dream

They go.

The docks of New Orleans. Margery enters, wearing a cape.

MARGERY (*to us*) Doña Athene sailed up to my husband's
plantation hissing all these seeds of suspicion in Pincepousse's
brain. "Come back to New Orleans. Things ain't what they

seem." I ups and escape back here to show Jacques my state. When he sees me, as I am, he'll love me then.

Margery goes. Enter Jacques Cornet, Dr. T, and Murmur.

JACQUES CORNET That steerage filled with people of the Indies haunts me. Do I just sit here?

DR. T That's one way. But let your thoughts inform your actions.

JACQUES CORNET Is courage that simple?

MURMUR My master comes to a shocking conclusion.

JACQUES CORNET Why am I moved? Those men and women were me. Is what I feel "love"? This love seems not to be a weakness but rather the beginning of a strength. How odd? Love? I must free my slaves. Yes, Murmur, you will be free.

MURMUR Will be? Why not: *are* free?

JACQUES CORNET Yes! *Are* free.

MURMUR Well, I'll be. This is how it happens. *(to us)* Act one. Scene one. Exit Murmur. Goodbye then.

Murmur starts to go. Margery appears and leaps on Jacques Cornet's back.

MARGERY Here I am!

JACQUES CORNET Oh god. Murmur, get rid of her.

Murmur pulls Margery off Jacques Cornet. Pincepousse enters.

PINCEPOUSSE What were you doing with my wife in your arms?

JACQUES CORNET She was on my back. Why would I want a woman in my arms?

PINCEPOUSSE Doctor, is this man as unmanned as he said?

73

DR. T   I've rarely seen a stallion smoothed into such a gelding.

MARGERY   It's not true! He's a true man and a great man!

JACQUES CORNET   She's hell's own jack in the box! Take her away!

MARGERY   I love you! Bud, look at me! Land ho!

Doña Athene enters, now mad, banging on a drum.

DOÑA ATHENE   Citizens of New Orleans! Hear me! A liar breathes in your midst! The self-proclaimed eunuch, Jacques Cornet? Hah! Unveil yourself!

The people of New Orleans appear.

HARCOURT   What's going on?

SPARKS   What's happening?

DORILANTE   What's she saying?

JACQUES CORNET   The woman's mad.

PINCEPOUSSE   You swear he's no man?

DR. T   I've told you—

MARGERY   He's what I've been told is a man.

LADY HARCOURT   The man is a eunuch.

MRS. SPARKS   Everyone knows that.

MME. DORILANTE   The blank spaces of the universe lie between his legs.

DOÑA SMERELDA   Who is this man? Are you new in town?

DOÑA ATHENE   Women of New Orleans, you married whores have duped your husbands in the past and shall again in a second when you learn his secret! He is whole! You will implore this monster to transform you back into whores!

LADY HARCOURT How dare you!

DOÑA ATHENE —as he has lain with you—and you and you!

MORALES Not with my wife! Jacques Cornet is my dearest friend.

DORILANTE He's my best friend.

HARCOURT Mine!

SPARKS Mine!

DOÑA ATHENE Horn-ed men of New Orleans, don't feign incredulity! Jacques Cornet has purchased entry into your trust.

JACQUES CORNET The woman's mad.

DOÑA ATHENE Ask her, the one with the microscope!

DOÑA POLISSENA I swear I don't know him.

DOÑA ATHENE Don't know him? I have seen you and him this very day make the undulating beast with two backs. (*attacking Doña Polissena*) You have driven a knife into my wifely heart as he sails out from his home into your secret doors.

DOÑA POLISSENA I do not know the man! Imprison the wench for slander!

MARGERY No! He is a man who has filled my sails with child.

PINCEPOUSSE A child!

MARGERY I call Jacques Cornet Messiah. I'm carrying his baby!

Margery throws off her cloak. Is she pregnant?

JACQUES CORNET Then it must be a virgin birth for I know not the woman.

PINCEPOUSSE   But you're my wife! I have a contract that says so.

MARGERY   But you're not my husband the way he is.

MORALES (*to Jacques Cornet*)   Did you not have a clavisectomy?

HARCOURT   Your key to the city was not shot off?

JACQUES CORNET   Why would Dr. Toutou lie?

DR. T   I ask myself that question everyday.

MARGERY   It's true.

MORALES   But I am your heir!

DORILANTE   I am his heir!

SPARKS   I have the will! I am the heir!

MORALES   Have you made fools of us all?

DOÑA SMERALDA   And I shall happily make a fool of you again! Take me, Jacques. If you are whole, then I sacrifice everything for you!

MRS. SPARKS   Yes! I surrender my secret!

LADY HARCOURT   I love Jacques Cornet!

MME. DORILANTE   You are my new world!

DOÑA POLISSENA   In the interest of science! I am yours!

The men and their wives advance on Jacques Cornet.

DOÑA SMERALDA   We

LADY HARCOURT   Shall

MRS. SPARKS   Not

DOÑA POLISSENA   Be

DOÑA SMERALDA AND THE WIVES   Denied!

JACQUES CORNET Stay back!

CREUX Don't I satisfy you, my dear?

MORALES Dr. Toubib, did you lie to me?

DR. T Let me explain—

MORALES (*drawing his sword*) Arrest Dr. Toubib!

JACQUES CORNET Unhand him!

The men draw their swords. Jacques Cornet wrests a sword from Creux and challenges the men. They parry.

MORALES Stop! Before we extract punishment, I announce a decision. Thanks to my rage, I rescind the right of deposit on the Mississippi. No ships may dock in New Orleans.

HARCOURT But it's our life blood!

DORILANTE The town will starve!

SPARKS You'll destroy the city!

MORALES When you starve, point the world's finger to Jacques Cornet! The Mississippi is closed!

Jacques Cornet frees Dr. T with elaborate sword play. Exit Jacques Cornet, Murmur, and Dr. T, pursued by the men.

DR. T (*to us*) Before we escape into the bayou, know what happened up north, when this news reached Washington.

Enter Jefferson and Meriwether.

MERIWETHER Send in troops to liberate the Mississippi!

JEFFERSON No! That will force England to join the fray. We have to get New Orleans legally before there's war. No word from Livingston? Bring me James Monroe.

JAMES MONROE *appears.*

JEFFERSON   Go to Paris. Join Livingston. I authorize you to spend ten million dollars—

MONROE   Ten million dollars?!

JEFFERSON   Ten million dollars to buy New Orleans.

MONROE   Buy New Orleans?!

JEFFERSON   Buy New Orleans. Move quickly! France is vulnerable. The future destiny of this republic depends on you!

Exit Jefferson, Meriwether and Monroe. Livingston appears.

LIVINGSTON   Monroe coming to Paris! I'll buy New Orleans before Monroe arrives. I'm going to be the only one in the history books.

Exit Livingston.

The bayou. Drums beat madly. Morales, Pincepousse, the women of New Orleans search for Jacques and go. Jacques, Murmur, and Dr. T emerge from hiding.

JACQUES CORNET   We must cleverly escape from the present misfortune. Murmur, you shall put on my clothes while I . . .

MURMUR   Sir, you'd expose me to be killed in your clothes?

JACQUES CORNET   Happy is the servant who has the glory of dying for his master.

MURMUR   I thought you freed me.

JACQUES CORNET   To demonstrate my affection, I shall free my favorite last. Who's there? Who comes?

Pincepousse appears, holding sword and lamp.

JACQUES CORNET   Ahhh, my brother.

PINCEPOUSSE   You dare call me brother?

78

JACQUES CORNET (*drawing his sword*)   My father was your father.

They duel.

PINCEPOUSSE   Your mother was his slave. Bought and sold for a very trivial price. I only tolerate you because of my compassion for a man who made three mistakes in his life. He left France for New Orleans. He had a weakness for women of color.

JACQUES CORNET   And his third mistake?

PINCEPOUSSE   He did not strangle the mistakes he made with those women *at birth*.

JACQUES CORNET   You honor him when you honor me.

PINCEPOUSSE (*attacking him*)   Sharing my wife's favors was not included in the honoraria. Fool! Learn how madly you rush on death!

They cross swords. Margery appears and cries out. Pincepousse turns to her. Jacques makes one home thrust mortally wounding him.

PINCEPOUSSE   I yield existence—a wife's honor's worth— life—its price—proves none too dear—truth, I did love her.

Pincepousse dies. Jacques Cornet wipes his sword.

JACQUES CORNET   Ridiculing the price of my mother.

MARGERY   Sire, now I am yours!

JACQUES CORNET   Leave me. I'll give you money for your child.

DR. T   Where will you go?

JACQUES CORNET (*taking out his maps*)   These maps lead me into *terra incognita*. The hieroglyphs of geography.

DR. T   You have no warmth. You can't wear these slippers.

JACQUES CORNET   As nature has given me my precious instincts, so I trust nature to care for me.

MURMUR   Do you want me to come with you? Please say no.

JACQUES CORNET   I'm become Robinson Crusoe. I want no man's company.

MURMUR   Thank god.

JACQUES CORNET   It shall be like stepping off a mountain into a white cloud.

DR. T   And Jacques Cornet goes into the white spaces.

Jacques Cornet goes. The townsmen and women enter to find Pincepousse's body.

SPARKS   Find Cornet!

HARCOURT   Bring him back!

PYTHAGORE   Death to Cornet!

MARGERY   Will he come back? What will become of me?

They go.

A large map of North America descends. Enter Napoleon in full majesty and Talleyrand.

NAPOLEON   Le Clerc dead? Our entire fleet wiped out. Damn sugar, damn coffee, damn the muslins of my wife! That American—the deaf one—

TALLYRAND   The one who wanted to buy New Orleans? Livingston.

NAPOLEON   Bring him here.

TALLYRAND   You can't sell New Orleans. I won't allow it.

NAPOLEON   You won't allow. I've listened to your slime long enough. Sell all of Louisiana. Get rid of all of it. I am no longer paltry, Citizen First Counsel. I will be Emperor!

TALLYRAND   Sell the entire Louisiana territory and risk making the United States a rival?

DR. T   And listen to what Napoleon says!

NAPOLEON   At first, America will be proud of their size. They'll start singing songs about their country—(*A scratchy recording of a choir singing "America the Beautiful"*).   I see slavery spreading like a cancer. I see this territory tearing blacks and whites apart. The poor United States—not prepared for greatness. Sell it. Get their money. Then we attack and destroy Britain. France, ruler of the seas, sails to an emasculated North America and reclaims war-torn Louisiana for France. (*The enormous white space of the Louisiana Territory glows on the map of North America.*)   Give them all this size. No country can be this big and survive. They'll collapse within three years. The luck of Napoleon will see me through.

Napoleon stands in shadows. Livingston appears.

DR. T   On April 11, 1803, the day before Monroe arrives—

TALLYRAND   I offer you all of Louisiana.

LIVINGSTON (*to us*)   Don't blink an eye. He's like Mephistopheles offering Faust the world. All this ours? Jefferson sent me here to buy only this little bit. Jefferson never imagined—if only I could talk to Jefferson.

TALLYRAND   Give me a price.

LIVINGSTON   Since no one knows what's there, four million dollars.

TALLYRAND   Twenty million francs? No, no, no, no. Fifty million francs.

LIVINGSTON   Ten million dollars for this? Out of the question.

Napoleon steps into the light.

NAPOLEON   Stop! Irresolution and deliberation are no longer in season. I renounce Louisiana. Take it or leave it.

Napoleon and Talleyrand go. Enter Monroe.

MONROE   Monroe arrives.

LIVINGSTON   Damn, I'll have to share the history books. I tell him the offer.

MONROE   How big is all this?

LIVINGSTON   Roughly nine hundred thousand square miles.

MONROE   Nine hundred thousand—

LIVINGSTON   What would we do, transformed into this Goliath?

MONROE   Megatherian.

LIVINGSTON   Herculean.

MONROE   We're a sensible Puritan country.

LIVINGSTON   We only require New Orleans.

MONROE   On the other hand. Look at the size of France.

LIVINGSTON   Look at the size of England.

MONROE   We'd be so big, the world would fear us—

LIVINGSTON   —cower before us.

LIVINGSTON AND MONROE   Let's do it.

Enter Napoleon and Talleyrand.

NAPOLEON   Get one hundred million francs.

TALLYRAND   I now need one hundred million francs.

MONROE Bargain bargain bargain . . .

LIVINGSTON Haggle haggle bargain . . .

MONROE We agree to sixty million francs plus twenty million francs for merchant claims—

LIVINGSTON Roughly fifteen million dollars.

NAPOLEON Done!

DR. T (*to us*) And this is how empires stumble into being.

Enter the Infanta, Doña Polissena, Toussaint.

INFANTA A hungry one-eyed Princess in Italy.

DOÑA POLISSENA A tiny mosquito in the Indies.

TOUSSAINT A former slave who challenged an empire and won. I died in France in a dungeon at the same time as these negotiations.

They go. Enter Jefferson and Meriwether.

JEFFERSON The news of the purchase reaches me on the Fourth of July 1803!—What! Fifteen million dollars???

DR. T Which in 2010 is worth roughly one hundred and ninety five million dollars.

JEFFERSON Fifteen million dollars???

DR. T As Linnaeus sent out young men to catalog the world's flora, so Mr. Jefferson liberates Meriwether Lewis from his desk, sending him out with William Clark to see what the hell it is they have bought.

Meriwether enters in full exploration gear.

JEFFERSON Meriwether, prepare to voyage into whiteness.

Jefferson goes. Music. Eerie. Majestic. Full of wonder. Meriwether moves onto an empty stage now blinding white.

A Figure appears in the distance, covered in bear skins huddled against the cold.

MERIWETHER   Hello? What tribe you from? I speak bit of Mandan. I'm separated from my party. You like pocket mirror? See self. Beads? Silk ribbons. Ivory comb. Tobacco. Tomahawk that can be pipe. Vermilion face paint.
(taking out list)
How long do Indians live?
How do you treat small pox?
Diseases of venery.
What kind of animals do you keep?
What kind of games do you play?
Does the Missouri flow northwest? Southwest? Or just west?
I have food? Tasty beef and eggs and vegetables boiled into a paste? M-m-m-m! You want?

The Figure tosses back the bear skin. It is Jacques Cornet, ragged, unshaven, his hair grown out.

JACQUES CORNET   No *foie gras?*

MERIWETHER   *Foie gras?*

JACQUES CORNET   I have a yen for *foie gras.* Like a song that refuses to vacate one's head, so was I sitting here thinking of Bourdeaux geese having grain stuffed down their throats to engorge their livers. Let me see that pocket mirror. I look a fright. Let me have some of that vermilion war paint. (*Jacques Cornet smears it on.*)   Yes, it appears I speak English.

MERIWETHER   What kind of Indian are you?

JACQUES CORNET   Descended from a tribe of fops that landed here a thousand years ago. We keep the good things of life alive. Music. Fashion. Let me try that paste—I'll eat it cold.

MERIWETHER (*passing him food*)   Who are you?

JACQUES CORNET   An inept traveler. (*eats*)   Your food is this dreadful at the beginning of a journey? This is food for the end of a journey.

MERIWETHER   Are you a citizen of the United States?

JACQUES CORNET   N.O. Letters which are also the initials of New Orleans. I am *Orleanais*. I believe there's a price on my head? Have you come to capture me and claim the reward?

Jacques Cornet seizes the tomahawk on Meriwether's belt.

MERIWETHER   Are you mad?

JACQUES CORNET   I'd have to be. To find myself in a blizzard dressed like this. Do you have whiskey with you? How big is your party?

Meriwether gives him a flask of whiskey. Jacques Cornet drinks.

MERIWETHER   So far we have twenty-two men plus three sergeants. My partner, William Clark, has brought the slave he's had from childhood. His name is York. Do you know him?

JACQUES CORNET   York? No. Why would I?

MERIWETHER   It always surprises me all Negroes don't know each other.

JACQUES CORNET   Being mulatto, I only know half the Negroes. Where are we?

MERIWETHER (*unfolding a map*)   In the Indiana territory. At the junction of the Mississippi and the Ohio rivers.

JACQUES CORNET   A collector of maps. As am I. Are we in white space yet?

Jacques Cornet reveals his cache of maps.

MERIWETHER We are on the brink! May I see? (*looks at the maps, then, amazed*) Would you join us? We're still building our party.

JACQUES CORNET Do you travel with women?

MERIWETHER Not yet.

JACQUES CORNET I'll stay here. If I discovered the river to India, I'd have to share it with you and I don't share.

MERIWETHER There is no sharing. The United States owns all this.

JACQUES CORNET This land is Spain's. Or that of France.

MERIWETHER Don't you know what happened? President Jefferson announced the purchase last Fourth of July. France sold all of Louisiana to us. Mr. Jefferson sent us out the next day to learn what we bought.

JACQUES CORNET What month is it now?

MERIWETHER November 1803.

JACQUES CORNET 1803? Has it been that long? When do the United States take over my city?

MERIWETHER This December.

JACQUES CORNET *Le code noir?* What about slavery?

MERIWETHER Read this.

Meriwether hands Jacques Cornet a document.

JACQUES CORNET "... these truths ... self-evident ... all men are created equal, ... endowed by their Creator with certain unalienable rights ... life, liberty and the pursuit of happiness ..."

MERIWETHER Slavery will end. After four hundred years of hoping, we'll find the western waterway. The world is

86

falling into place. Go back home. Be part of the new world's bravery.

JACQUES CORNET   Might it be safe to go back? Pincepousse? I killed him in a perfectly legitimate duel. Yes! I'll write to my quasi-former slave, Cupidon Murmur. Do you have paper?

Meriwether gives him paper and pencil.

JACQUES CORNET (*writes*)   "Open my house. Put out my wardrobe. Alert Mme. Mandragola. Tell no one you have heard from me, not even Dr. Toutou. I want my arrival to be a surprise! Your former master, now friend, Jacques Cornet." Can you post it for me. (*Meriwether takes the letter*)   I tell you New Orleans is paradise.

MERIWETHER   If it was paradise before, imagine what it shall be now.

JACQUES CORNET   You'll solve the puzzle of the white spaces. We'll meet again!

Jacques Cornet flings his bear skins onto Meriwether and goes. Meriwether Lewis waves goodbye to Jacques and recedes into the distance.

Darkness.

A trumpet plays. The Spanish flag is lowered. Morales enters.

MORALES   On this day in November 1803, Spain gives Louisiana to France. We lower the Spanish flag—

The French flag is raised.

DORILANTE   And raise the French flag. We lower the French flag.

The French flag lowers. Jacques Cornet enters.

JACQUES CORNET   I return to New Orleans. *A Free Man of Color Comes Home.* I'm back within the pages of my play.—

87

Nothing has changed! Out on the river, I see a score of ships anchored. It's so quiet—

Murmur appears, carrying a picnic hamper.

JACQUES CORNET   Murmur! I told you to meet me at home

MURMUR   You want to be here, sir. Look! American war ships waiting for the flags to be swapped.

JACQUES CORNET   The flag of the United States rises as I arrive? Sometimes I am overwhelmed by the impeccability of my timing. Murmur! Good man! Did you miss me?

MURMUR   Yes, sire.

JACQUES CORNET   I missed you.

MURMUR   Very good, sir.

JACQUES CORNET   What's wrong?

MURMUR   Nothing. I've brought you food.

JACQUES CORNET   A New Orleans feast! Sherry! Chicken! *Etoufée!* Tell Doctor T I'm home! Set another place! Add one for you. Join us—

MURMUR *(setting the places)*   It was discovered that Dr. Toubib had fled Boston as a slave. His owner reclaimed him and took him away.

JACQUES CORNET   Dr. Toubib reclaimed? But that's not in my play.

NUNS *dressed in black pass by, eyes down, hands in prayer.*

JACQUES CORNET   But I know them—

MURMUR   Doña Smeralda, slain by her husband.
Doña Polissena, dead of the plague.

Doña Athene, Lady Harcourt, Mme. Dorilante and Mrs. Sparks, abandoned by their husbands and foresworn by you, had nowhere to go.

DOÑA ATHENE   We joined into an order of penitents called *Slaves of the Unquenchable Lust of Mary Magdalene.*

JACQUES CORNET   Why are you here?

DOÑA ATHENE   To witness your fate.

THE NUNS (*sing*)   Repent!

The Nuns go.

JACQUES CORNET   Repent? No! Long live the pretty girls! The wine cup! The glory of Earth's merry ball! Throw off your habits! We are in an Illyrian time. The golden age begins! Raise the American flag! Hurry! Let the freedom begin! Why isn't the flag ascending? Who is in charge of raising the flag?

Murmur turns, terrified. The Ghost of Pincepousse enters.

GHOST OF PINCEPOUSSE   Jacques, didst thou invite me to thy banquet?

JACQUES CORNET   My brother, I am glad to see death has not prevented us from having a conversation on this historic day. I plead a favor. Would you testify that I killed thee in a perfectly conventional duel between honorable men? You're dead so what difference can it make? Speak, speak! I am longing to know your purpose.

GHOST OF PINCEPOUSSE   I have come to witness your destruction.

JACQUES CORNET   I'm not destroyed. I lead a long, happy life. Look—the flag catches the wind!

The American flag fills the stage. The Ghost of Pincepousse clutches Jacques' arm as Sparks, Harcourt and Dorilante seize Jacques Cornet and put him in shackles.

MURMUR *(calls out)* Take him!

JACQUES CORNET Release me! What madness is this?

SPARKS Good work, Murmur.

Sparks gives Murmur a bag of coins.

JACQUES CORNET You betrayed me?

MURMUR The price of your reward was the exact cost for me to buy my freedom.

JACQUES CORNET But I gave you your freedom.

MURMUR They guaranteed it! You're real good at dangling carrots of freedom in front of a donkey who's pushing your crates and cleaning your clothes and fetching your women and then vanishing into a swamp, taking my freedom with you. I'm well-versed in all your lessons, Jacques Cornet.
"Born to myself, I like myself alone."
I've learned to spray myself with your cologne.
Betray you? I merely earned my price.
I am now a free man of color. I find that *very* nice.

Exit Murmur.

SPARKS Let the auction begin!

JACQUES CORNET What is being auctioned?

SPARKS You.

JACQUES CORNET Let me be clearheaded. Let me go home. Let me get my papers. Let me understand what you're saying—

SPARKS It's very simple. The United States government now controls your property.

HARCOURT   We're here to dispose of your property.

SPARKS   To dispose of you.

JACQUES CORNET   I'm not property.

SPARKS   You are mulatto.

JACQUES CORNET   But in New Orleans that is applauded!

SPARKS   We live in a newer Orleans.

JACQUES CORNET   But you are *mamelouc*—you quadroon—

SPARKS   You'd never know it.

DORILANTE   Fate favored our skin.

JACQUES CORNET   But this is my play.

SPARKS   There is now a new playwright. Reality. Here are your new pages. (*He gives Jacques Cornet a new script.*)   Let the auction begin.

The men advance on Jacques Cornet.

JACQUES CORNET (*shaking them off*)   Look at that flag! New Orleans is now part of the United States of America, where all men are created equal!

SPARKS   Let's start the bidding.

JACQUES CORNET   You cannot buy what is not for sale. Look at me. My arms and legs find echoes in marbled ancient Greeks. Such perfection is for the Acropolis, not for your tawdry hands. This is insanity. I return home after many months exploring and this is my welcome committee? Surely you joke. Surely. Surely. This is not the France of Louis *Quatorze*. *Le Code Noir* is one hundred years out of date. This is New Orleans. People do not behave this way. I have a document here that fueled my return. Read these words. The man who wrote this is president. I demand to see the man who wrote *Life, Liberty, and the Pursuit of Happiness.* I demand he appear and correct this outrageous—This is my play! I summon you!

Jefferson appears.

JEFFERSON   This is most unusual.

JACQUES CORNET   Sir, these inhuman men are under the impression they can buy me as if I were a cow.

DORILANTE   Inhuman? Hath not a slave owner eyes?

SPARKS   Hath not a slave owner hands?

DORILANTE   Organs?

HARCOURT   Dimensions?

SPARKS   Senses?

HARCOURT   Fed with the same food?

SPARKS   Hurt with the same weapons?

DORILANTE   Subject to the same diseases?

JACQUES CORNET   Sir, I am a free man who lives as a free man—

JEFFERSON   Let me settle this humanely. Go. You'll have your turn.

DORILANTE   Remember, if you prick us, do we not bleed?

SPARKS   If you tickle us, do we not laugh?

HARCOURT   If you poison us, do we not die?

DORILANTE   If you wrong us, shall we not . . .

MEN   . . . revenge?

They go.

JACQUES CORNET   I apologize—usually I am of a calmer mien. Let me identify myself. Jacques Cornet. New Orleans.

JEFFERSON   Was your father Pierre Cornet? *Le Duc de Pincepousse*? I knew him in Paris. He went to New Orleans for his fortune.

JACQUES CORNET   And I am part of the fortune he found.

JEFFERSON   For a time we each pursued the same woman. One of us was victorious. I forget which. I was sorry to learn of his death.

JACQUES CORNET   It was peaceful.

JEFFERSON   We can wish for no more.

JACQUES CORNET   No more than wishing my life to continue in peace.

JEFFERSON   Your mother? Someone I assume he met on his plantation?

JACQUES CORNET   I did not know my mother. She was sold after my birth.

JEFFERSON   And you were given your freedom.

JACQUES CORNET   Earned my freedom. In New Orleans, you'll see iron wrought into vines, decorating each building. I instituted that factory. I have a talent for alchemy. That's how I purchased my freedom.

JEFFERSON   You're an impressive man.

JACQUES CORNET   All the reason more why you must resolve this situation. I'm not extolling my virtues. I'm stating my rights. You wrote All men are created equal. New Orleans is now part of the United States. Those words are law.

JEFFERSON   Unfortunately, my words are not part of the Constitution. The Constitution is where we keep the laws.

93

JACQUES CORNET   And where you do keep the laws on
slavery?

JEFFERSON   The Constitution doesn't really mention slavery.
My words were merely part of a Declaration to a King telling
him what we wanted.

JACQUES CORNET   Should I then write a letter to you
declaring my desire?

JEFFERSON   I could imagine what it would be.

JACQUES CORNET   And would I be wrong?

JEFFERSON   Slavery is a terrible thing.

JACQUES CORNET   Then bring these men in and advise
them—

JEFFERSON   It started so simply. People in the Carolinas
growing cotton—tobacco—sugar—coffee. People around
the world wanting our crops. Demand increases. We need to
expand. Georgia. Tennessee. Kentucky. Not enough people
living here to work the land, to tend, to harvest, who can
endure the heat. We have to import workers. That's how it
starts. It grows and grows and grows—

JACQUES CORNET   You make African dealings sound like a
stroll through the market.

JEFFERSON   It is a market. A crazed market. Have you ever seen
a man addicted to opium? So it is with a world now addicted
to our produce. We're all addicts. We need more slaves. The
world needs our goods. We need the money to build a
capitol, a house for the president to live in, to buy Louisiana.
We live off the labors of those possessions and can't let go. We
are the slaves to slavery.

JACQUES CORNET   You keep slaves and hate slavery. Are you a
hypocrite?

JEFFERSON   Jesus, who some say was the kindest man who ever lived—

JACQUES CORNET   We weren't talking about Jesus.

JEFFERSON   When defending one's self, one always quotes Jesus. In all the Four Testaments, never once does Jesus mention slavery. If the possible Messiah can't bring up the subject, how can I?

JACQUES CORNET   You keep several hundred slaves at Monticello.

JEFFERSON   How many slaves on your plantation?

JACQUES CORNET   When I get back home, I will free my slaves.

JEFFERSON   How will they survive?

JACQUES CORNET   Like me, they will find their strength.

JEFFERSON   Do you not think that your strength comes from your father?

JACQUES CORNET   You mean, my *white* blood? My blood is my blood. I do not live in fractions. I demand that you act.

JEFFERSON   Have faith. The world always balances itself.

JACQUES CORNET   But when?

JEFFERSON   Patience. It'll happen. Have faith. "This abomination must have an end." I'm on your side! Hang on!

JACQUES CORNET   When you're in bed with your dead wife's slave who was also her half-sister, do you woo the dusky Miss Sally, your bronze Venus, with the joys of patience?

JEFFERSON   I refuse to be put on trial in a court of your contrivance.

JACQUES CORNET   Were you patient buying the mountaintop where you built your home? Did you say I really don't have the money. I'll wait until later. Hang on! Hang on? A gallows hangs on. You have such faith in the beneficence of the future that you need no faith in today. Mr. Jefferson, why wait! Why not deal with it now when you have the power! All I ask is that you listen to your own words. Make your words real. Change the future now. You'll avoid a Civil War— Jim Crow—Dred Scott—lynching—back of the bus—whites only—assassination—degradation—

JEFFERSON   I really don't like confrontation. I like to take quiet walks under the fig trees and experience the present. The "now" is where we are now. I'm comfortable in the now. Try it. Say Now.

The men appear.

JACQUES CORNET   Get back! They can't own me.

JEFFERSON   I'm afraid they can.

JACQUES CORNET   Thomas Jefferson. The third president of the United States who wrote the Declaration of Independence. Are you out of your fucking mind!

Jacques Cornet rolls the Declaration of Independence into a ball and hurls it at Jefferson.

JEFFERSON   Excellent to be with you tonight. "All men are created equal." Sometimes I curse writing those words. I did write other phrases I thought as winning.

JACQUES CORNET   Don't go!

Exit Jefferson. The men advance on Jacques Cornet.

JACQUES CORNET   Back! This is still my play. I summon Meriwether Lewis.

Meriwether enters, in bear skins. A terrible change has befallen him.

JACQUES CORNET   My friend from the white spaces! I've reconsidered your kind invitation to join your Corps of Discovery. In spite of your paste of boiled beef and the absence of women, I and my maps will happily join you in the pages of history! Tell these men—(*He looks at pages of the new script*)   No. this cannot be. It says this is the last night of your life. But you're a success! Your journey—

MERIWETHER   Some of it is majestic. Some of it is bleak. But the truth is there's no direct water route across this continent.

JACQUES CORNET   No western waterway?

MERIWETHER   Mountains sprang up to obstruct the water. Then, flat land.

JACQUES CORNET   Your expedition a failure?

MERIWETHER   People think everything a failure. People thought the purchase of Louisiana a failure. I kept hanging on.

JACQUES CORNET   Hang on! Hang on! Hang on! Your Corps of Discovery made no discovery?

MERIWETHER   Our boundaries. Is it really the last night of my life?

Jacques Cornet looks at the new script and nods.

MERIWETHER   No matter. Tell me the circumstances of the scene?

JACQUES CORNET   It says you're staying at a shabby inn outside Nashville. You've been drinking, taking drugs. Your sense of failure is overwhelming.

MERIWETHER   Who kills me?

JACQUES CORNET   You.

MERIWETHER   Oh. (*Meriwether takes the new script and reads flatly*)   "I failed Jefferson. I didn't find the passage to the sea." Let me try that again (*with emotion*). "I failed Jefferson. I didn't find the passage to the sea. Four hundred years of explorers' dreams . . . Columbus, Magellan, me."

JACQUES CORNET   The innkeeper calls out: I will make your bed.

MERIWETHER   I don't want feathers. I can only sleep on the floor. "Stage directions. He spreads his buffalo robe and bear skins on the floor."

JACQUES CORNET   (*he makes that whistle of seduction*)   I step out of the azaleas. Hear the sound of the mockingbird.

MERIWETHER   It's a sign of death when the mockingbird no longer mocks but speaks in his true voice.

JACQUES CORNET   This is what the mockingbird says in its true voice.

MERIWETHER   Failure. Our dreams once pulsed with the sexual charge of the unknown. Those dreams—now emasculated, thanks to me. I am a eunuch now that I lack my dreams.

JACQUES CORNET   We'll keep your secret. People will like you much better.

MERIWETHER   Good. Because the reality is there is no promised land. No! Don't tell me there is no promised land. Imagine going to the moon and finding nothing there.

JACQUES CORNET   Nothing. All my maps as worthless as Jefferson's words . . .

MERIWETHER   No! Keep the maps. Never give up the enormity of this dream. Keep telling the lie. The United States will always be the last undiscovered terrain—even if we have to move the white spaces inside our head. Always hold out the promise that you can find your passage to the west, to whatever it is—love everlasting, bottomless wealth, glory—

JACQUES CORNET   Freedom.

MERIWETHER   That dream must never die.

JACQUES CORNET   Nor must you! If that's how you stay alive, then tell yourself the lie!

MERIWETHER   I don't have that gift.

JACQUES CORNET   But I do! *A Free Man of Color or The Happy Life of a Man in Power. A Free Man of Color or How I Take Control. A Free Man of Color or How Jefferson Is a Liar. A Free Man of Color or How My Father Sold My Mother. A Free Man of Color or How Murmur Betrayed Me. A Free Man of Color or*—

MERIWETHER   The white spaces forever.

Meriwether shoots himself and dies.

SPARKS   Sold!

JACQUES CORNET   No!

Sparks advances and chains Jacques Cornet.

SPARKS   When I bought Pincepousse's estate at his death with all its chattel, I claimed Margery and her child as mine.

Margery appears.

MARGERY   He sold my child. I don't know where or to whom but he didn't sell me. He kept me in the house. Jacques Cornet worked out in the field. I never stopped loving Jacques. I never saw him.

Creux appears and stands over Jacques Cornet.

CREUX Oh United States, be watchful. If not, you'll have Santo Domingo all over again! Be vigilant or your Negroes will riot and rape your women. Hordes of crazed Othellos will debase our unwilling Desdemonas and then dance on your corpses whilst eating ribs and devouring slashes of bright red melons. Carve this image in eternity's stone: Bloody Toussaint is the definitive face of the Negro for all time! His rage shall never die! He wants you dead! Never lose your fear!

Murmur appears.

MURMUR One day, Jacques saw his way. He escaped and vanished into unknown spaces. He never saw his son.

Dr. T, in rags, appears.

DR. T Perhaps his son returned years later as Nat Turner, or as Malcolm—as any man who tried to make those words "All men are created equal" literal.

JACQUES CORNET I see visions of the future when generations of Margerys and Murmurs and Dr. Toubibs and the girls of Mme. Mandragola will be trapped on rooftops in New Orleans, reaching up to heaven to be saved. I say those bitter words "Hang on!" And while I hang, I think about a time when I had my maps, when I wrote my play, when New Orleans meant paradise . . .

Haydn Trio in G Major. Third Movement. The ghosts of the people of New Orleans in 1801 appear in half light amidst wreckage.

DORILANTE I mase double.

MME. MANDRAGOLA I set that.

SPARKS Mase double again!

MME. MANDRAGOLA I set that and I win!

MORALES   Jacques, have some consideration. I can't keep my wife waiting.

JACQUES CORNET (*looks at his chains*)   1801. The last time men dressed like this.

DR. T (*to us*)   Jacques Cornet. *A Free Man of Color or How One Man Became an American.*

THE END